Peter Fauland

Mastering the
Fujifilm X100T and X100S

rockynook

Peter Fauland
info@fauland-photography.com

Publisher: Scott Cowlin
Project Editor: Ted Waitt
Copyeditor: Jeanne Hansen
Translator: David Schlesinger
Layout: Anna Diechtierow
Cover Design: Anna Diechtierow
Printer: Versa Press, Inc. through Four Colour Print Group
Printed in the USA

ISBN 978-1-937538-80-4

1st Edition 2015
© 2015 by Peter Fauland

Rocky Nook Inc.
802 East Cota St., 3rd Floor
Santa Barbara, CA 93103
www.rockynook.com

Copyright © 2015 by dpunkt.verlag GmbH, Heidelberg, Germany.
Title of the German original: Das Fujifilm X100T / X100S Handbuch
ISBN 978-3-86490-249-9
Translation Copyright © 2015 by Rocky Nook. All rights reserved.

Library of Congress Cataloging-in-Publication Data

Fauland, Peter.
 [Fujifilm X100T/X100S Handbuch. English]
 Mastering the Fujifilm X100T and X100S / Peter Fauland. -- 1st Edition.
  pages cm
 ISBN 978-1-937538-80-4 (softcover : alk. paper)
 1. Fujifilm digital cameras--Handbooks, manuals, etc. I. Title.
 TR263.F85F3813 2015
 771.3'2--dc23
                            2015018394

About the Author

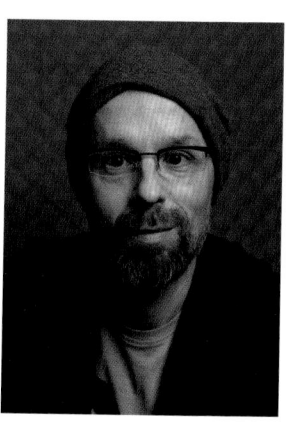

Peter Fauland is a professional photographer and teacher who leads workshops around the world for photography enthusiasts as well as for corporate clients. Originally from the school of classic black-and-white landscape film photography, Fauland now practices portrait, event, and architectural photography. While living in Switzerland and France for several years, he documented the construction of a complex detector system at CERN/the European Organization for Nuclear Research (Geneva) and he constructed a special hybrid camera consisting of a large-format camera system with a DSLR as the sensor. Fauland currently lives and works in Berlin, Germany. He believes the new generation of system cameras, such as those in the Fujifilm X-series, has brought the work of photography back to something intimate and direct. If he could work with only one camera, it would be from the X100 family.

Table of Contents

INTRODUCTION

*"It's well-balanced, feels great in your hand,
and makes working a simple pleasure."*

This quotation from a good friend of mine is not about
a camera, but about a knife. He's a professional chef
who spends at least eight hours in the kitchen every day.
Aside from sharpness, there are a variety of other qualities—shape, size, weight, and handling—that determine
how well a knife will accomplish a task.

As a photographer, I see a number of parallels in my
own work. In addition to various technical specifications,
a camera's size and weight and the arrangement of its
controls determine a lot about the way you shoot. Until
recently, small and compact cameras were primarily intended as entry-level models with no real applications
in more demanding photographic work. Digital single-lens
reflex (DSLR) camera systems intended for professional and
semiprofessional photographers were the only choice
for those with higher demands who needed to be able to

manage a variety of shooting situations. But the advent of mirrorless system cameras has fundamentally changed that. "I came for the size, I stayed for the quality," said photographer Matt Brandon regarding his decision to adopt a mirrorless system. His comment also perfectly summarizes my switch from a large, heavy DSLR system to the Fujifilm X-Series.

In the following chapters, I discuss both the Fujifilm X100S and the Fujifilm X100T from my perspective as a professional photographer. I cover countless ways of using both cameras, and I also point out their differences. *Mastering the Fuji X100* by Michael Diechtierow (also published by Rocky Nook, ISBN 978-1-933952-98-7) extensively covers the original X100, and I refer to the book a few times to elucidate minor points. I highly recommend Michael's book if you are looking for a thorough discussion of this early model.

The user manual that comes with the Fujifilm X100T is brief and addresses only the most essential functions of the camera. I recommend downloading the complete 300-page owner's manual from the Fujifilm website (see chapter 5, "Links"). I occasionally reference it in this book.

Even though I use several Fujinon XF fixed focal length and zoom lenses, as well as various Fujifilm X-Series cameras, the Fujifilm X100T and X100S have special significance for me. The lens, which is equivalent to a

35mm focal length in a 35mm camera format, perfectly suits my style of composing photographs for most shooting situations. This trait, in combination with its classic operation and compact size, was enough to win me over. The possibility of using conversion lenses to adjust the focal length to 28mm or 50mm (35mm equivalent) makes the X100 series ideal for travel, portrait, and documentary photography.

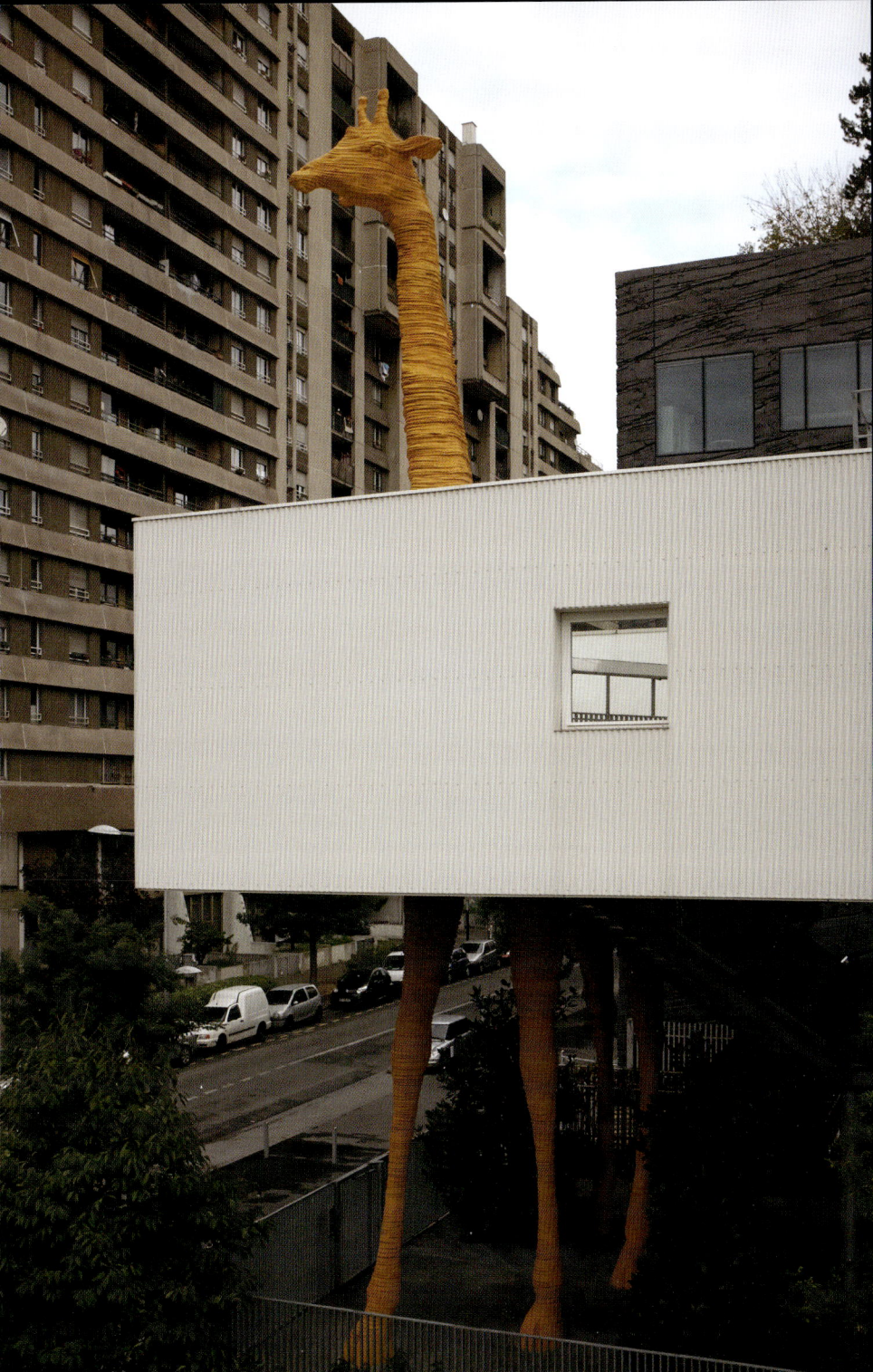

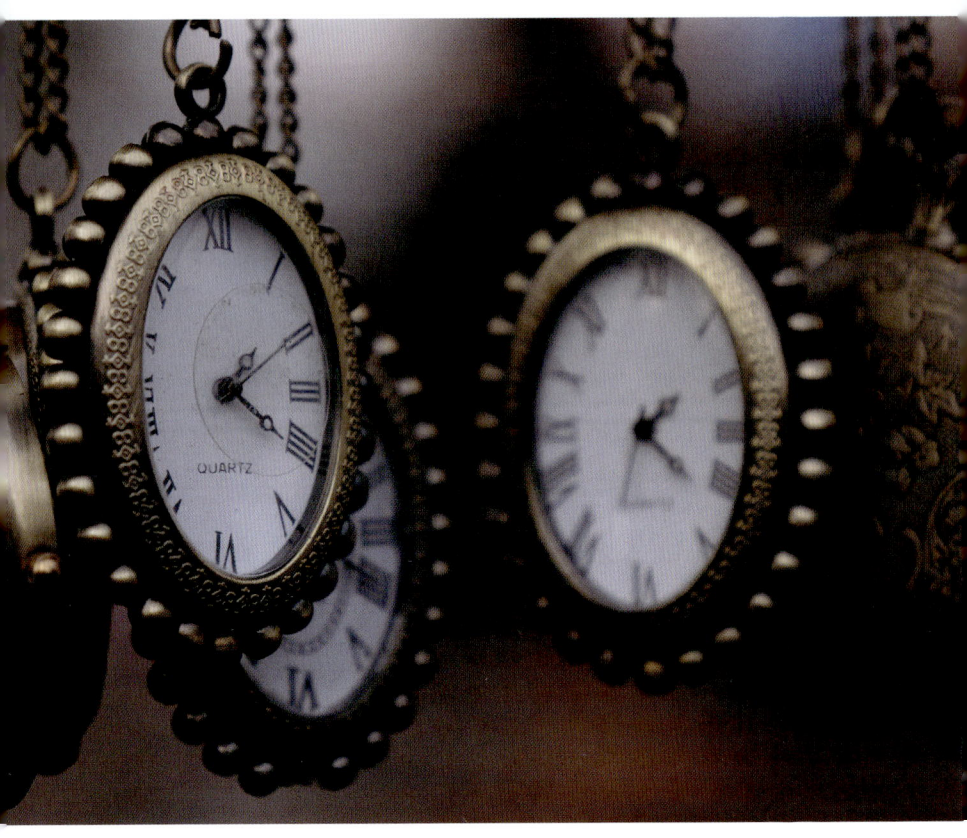

I THE RANGEFINDER CAMERA AND THE HISTORY OF THE X100 SERIES

In contrast with DSLR cameras, which deliver the image to the viewfinder through an optical system that includes a moveable mirror and a pentaprism, rangefinder cameras have an optical viewfinder and a focusing aid that are connected to the distance meter on the lens. On classic film rangefinder cameras, the focusing process usually involves a split image, with both images moving along a horizontal axis. When the images are perfectly aligned, the subject is in focus. In the days before autofocus, this was the standard way to adjust focus, and many modern digital cameras still use this approach for manual focus control.

Rangefinder cameras have both advantages and disadvantages compared to DSLR cameras. On the plus side, rangefinders don't need a complex mirror mechanism, so you can continuously view the scene through the viewfinder. This is an advantage particularly during long exposures. Another advantage of not having a mirror is that rangefinder cameras are not subject to vibrations that occur when the mirror swings out of the way, as it does in a DSLR—so camera shake is less of a problem at slow shutter speeds. When the shutter is released, rangefinder cameras make less noise than DSLRs, which can be a significant advantage in some shooting circumstances (e.g., during concerts or plays). A rangefinder's large, bright viewfinder also makes it possible to attain precise focus in poor lighting conditions. With a DSLR, it can be difficult to see the image through the viewfinder, and many autofocus systems are simply not capable of focusing sharply and quickly in low light. Yet another advantage is that rangefinders have a compact construction, which allows for a small flange focal distance. These qualities make rangefinder cameras easier to transport, quicker to prepare for a shot, and much less conspicuous than big DSLR systems. When I photograph speeches and other presentations with a rangefinder camera, for example, I often notice that speakers don't even realize they are being photographed. Working discreetly means being able to capture moments candidly and naturally.

The construction of the optics in rangefinder cameras causes the perspective of the viewfinder to be slightly different from the perspective of the lens. The difference between these two angles of view is called parallax. Parallax makes it impossible to adjust the image frame precisely when you are shooting with a small subject distance. The captured image will not be identical to the image that appears in the viewfinder—both the frame and the point of focus will be slightly different. Modern rangefinder cameras account for parallax by shifting the superimposed framing guides. The parallax compensation in the Fujifilm X100T and X100S displays an adjusted frame in the optical viewfinder that corresponds to the captured image. Parallax does not affect rangefinder cameras with electronic viewfinders because they use a true live image in the viewfinder.

The Fujifilm FinePix X100 was introduced in September 2010 at Photokina and became the first camera in what would become a very successful series of cameras. The X100 marries the classic design principles of traditional film cameras—mechanical dials for shutter speed, aperture, and exposure compensation—with a 12-megapixel CMOS sensor in a 2/3-inch format, an EXR Processor, a fast 23mm (35mm equivalent) prime lens, and a newly engineered hybrid viewfinder that allows photographers to toggle between optical and electronic views. With a 0.5x magnification, the viewfinder allows users to superimpose relevant exposure details, camera settings, and a framing window on a screen that automatically updates brightness as necessary. The electronic viewfinder has a resolution of 1.4 million pixels and offers a clear, bright image, even in dark situations and in macro mode.

The 23mm f/2 prime lens has eight elements in six groups, including one aspherical element. The nine-blade aperture diaphragm makes attractive bokeh possible at the maximum aperture. And the integrated neutral density (ND) filter that provides light reduction of three stops is easily accessible from either the camera menu or one of three assignable buttons.

When you use the electronic viewfinder, you have access to 49 autofocus (AF) areas. The size of each area can be changed. When you use the optical viewfinder, 25 AF areas are available.

The next-generation model, the Fujifilm X100S, became available in 2013. It features the APS-C X-Trans CMOS sensor, the well-known 16.3 megapixel image sensor that does not require a low-pass filter and is used in Fuji's X-Pro1 and X-E1 cameras. The X100S is powered by the new and improved EXR Processor II (offering processing speeds twice as fast as the EXR Processor) and features a further developed hybrid viewfinder paired with the same excellent 23mm f/2 prime lens.

By popular demand, the autofocus was drastically improved over the first X100 model, in large part due to the phase-detection pixels on the sensor. Depending on the shooting circumstances, you can use either contrast- or phase-detection autofocus. As the first truly digital rangefinder camera, the X100S also comes with a digital split-image display that allows users to employ the time-honored manual focusing techniques from the days of film. Focus peaking technology makes it possible to achieve precise focus and sharpness control. The electronic viewfinder offers 100% coverage with a resolution of 2.36 megapixels. Yet another new feature is the Q button, which allows for quick and easy access to some of the camera's most important settings.

X100

The functionality of the Q button became available for the X100 with the RAW button after a firmware update in late 2013.

THE HYBRID VIEWFINDER

The hybrid viewfinder is one of the signature features of the Fujifilm X100 camera series. Photographers can switch between the electronic viewfinder (EVF) and the optical viewfinder (OVF) by using a small lever near the lens on the front of the camera. Fujifilm introduced the third generation of this feature in September 2014 with the X100T.

X100T

One of the new features of the X100T is the ability to activate a small EVF window and focus peaking while using the OVF, which helps enable more precise focusing. See figure 1.1.

Viewfinder type	Hybrid viewfinder (optical and electronic)
Construction	Reverse Galilean viewfinder
Magnification	0.5x (OVF), 0.65x (EVF)
Coverage of frame area versus capture area	Approximately 92% (OVF)
EVF resolution	2,360,000 dots
Coverage of viewing area versus capture area	100% (EVF)
Rangefinder options	Split-image indicator, focus peaking, digital magnification
Diopter adjustment	−2 to +1

Table 1.1: **Hybrid viewfinder specifications**

The optimal viewfinder mode may depend on the shooting conditions and lighting; for example, your main priority may be to evaluate the ambient light in real time as you shoot, or it may be to establish precise focus.

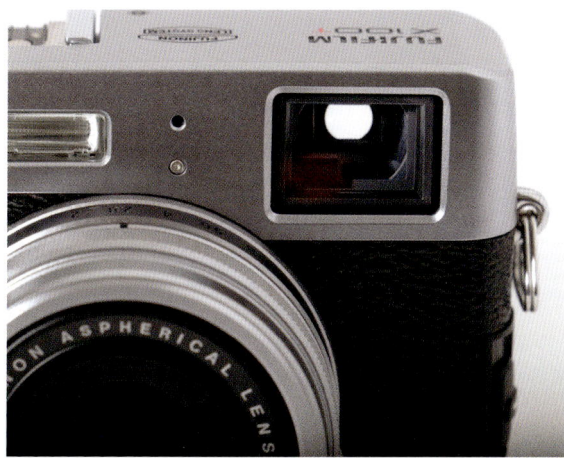

Figure 1.1: **The EVF overlay for the OVF, seen in the lower left of the viewfinder window (highlighted in red)**

   With the X100 and the X100S, when photographers focus manually they have to adjust each shot for parallax by pressing the shutter-release button halfway. With a coverage area of 92%, the optical viewfinder area of the X100T has increased by 2%. Other improvements to the OVF/EVF include the small indicators that rotate according to the camera's orientation and the ability to choose between viewing a natural image or a version that represents the current shooting settings, such as the application of a film simulation.

X100T

The hybrid viewfinder of the Fujifilm X100T offers real-time parallax adjustment while you use the optical viewfinder.

   The EVF frame rate is 54 frames per second, and its lag time is a modest 0.005 second, making it identical to the viewfinder in the Fujifilm X-T1, which provides a smooth live view.

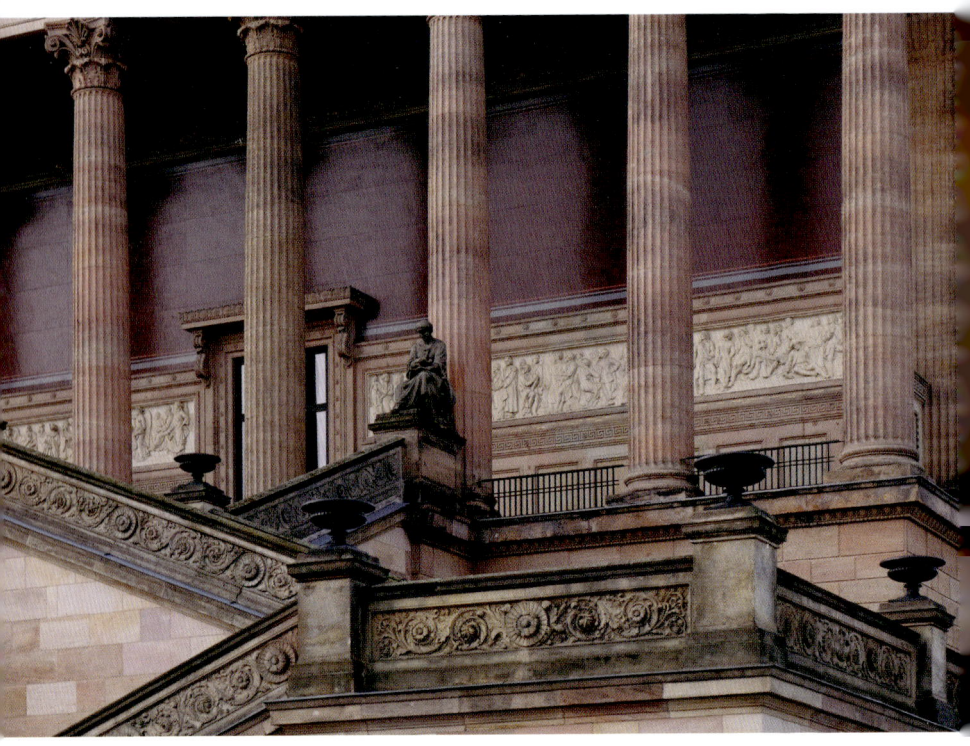

2 DESCRIPTION AND OPERATION OF THE CAMERA

UNPACKING AND GETTING READY

If you search for new camera models on YouTube, you'll find no shortage of unboxing videos—essentially boring clips of people unpacking their new cameras and revealing the factory-included accessories. The equipment that comes with the X100T includes an NP-95 rechargeable battery, a battery charger, a USB cable, and a shoulder strap. The camera takes SD, SDHC, or SDXC memory cards; at a minimum, they should be Class 10 (with a minimum 10 MB/second write speed), especially if you save your images as both RAW and JPEG files or if you use continuous shooting. An even better option is to use a Class 1 or Class 3 ultrahigh-speed (UHS) card (10 MB/second or 30 MB/second, respectively).

X100T

It takes roughly 3.5 hours to charge the battery for the first time. USB charging is another new feature that was introduced with the X100T.

If you use your computer to charge your battery via USB, be sure your computer doesn't automatically go to sleep because that may interrupt the charging process. The battery life indicator reveals how much charge is remaining: three bars is a full charge, two bars is between one-third and two-thirds of a full charge, one bar is no more than one-third of a full charge, and one blinking red bar means the camera will soon shut down. The jump from one bar to imminent shutdown can happen fairly quickly, so when you see one bar, it makes sense to load a spare battery (which I recommend purchasing).

Use the small diopter adjustment dial to adjust the viewfinder to your vision so you can see sharply through the viewfinder. When the indicators along the bottom edge of the window are as sharp as possible, you have found the optimal setting. It is particularly important to find the correct diopter setting to get the sharpest images possible if you plan to manually focus.

FIRMWARE UPDATES

Fujifilm regularly releases firmware updates for its cameras (see chapter 5, "Links"). These updates offer fixes and improvements for the camera's internal operating software and increase the range of the camera's functionality. Many updates are in response to comments from the ever-growing number of photographers who use Fujifilm gear.

It is easy to install updates. First, format your memory card, then save the downloaded DAT file to it. With the card in the camera, hold down the Display/Back button while you turn on your camera, and the firmware setup menu will appear. The current firmware status will be displayed along with the option to start or cancel the update. The battery must be fully charged before you start the update or you will not be able to proceed; if the update process is interrupted because of power loss, the camera will become inoperable and require professional servicing to bring it back to life. The update process lasts a few seconds. After it completes, turn your camera off, then on again, and the new software will be up and running. One final display screen indicates that the firmware update process was successful.

As of early 2015, there were no firmware updates for the X100T, which is why the illustrations in figure 2.1 display the process for the Fujifilm X-T1. The illustrations are functionally identical to the X100T process.

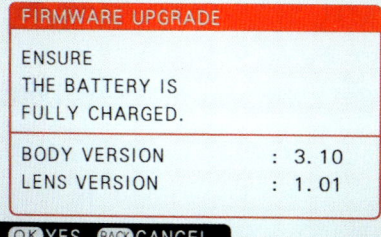

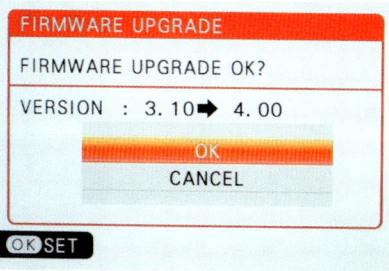

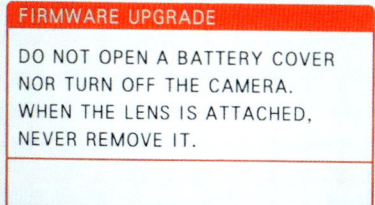

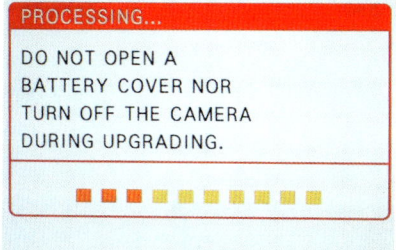

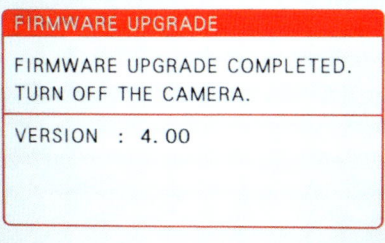

Figure 2.1: Firmware update

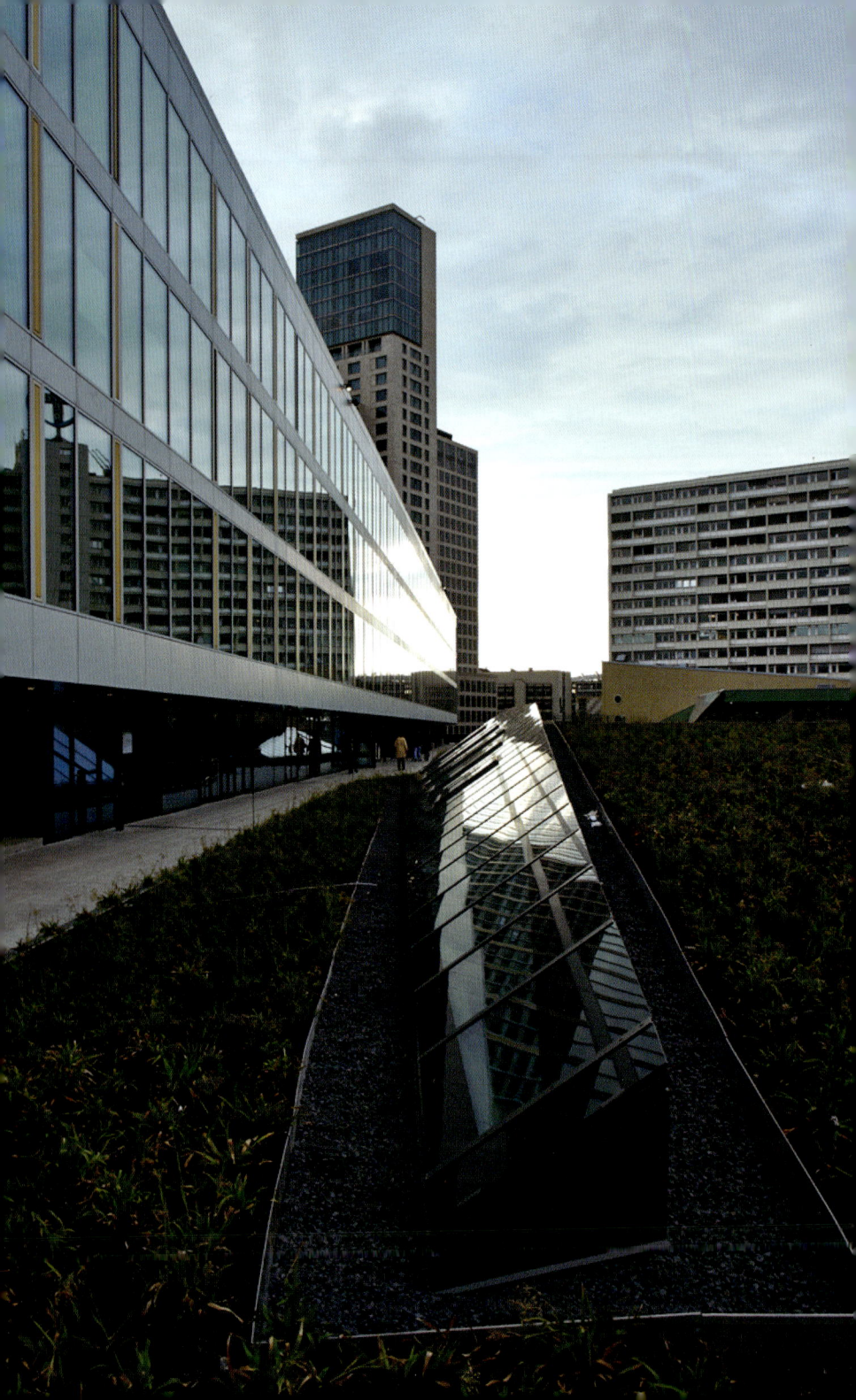

2.1 Operating the Camera

Before we get into the operation of the camera, let's go over the individual controls. Subsequent chapters will reference their names, and you can find a detailed explanation of them in the camera owner's manual (links to download the owner's manuals for the X100T and X100S are provided in chapter 5).

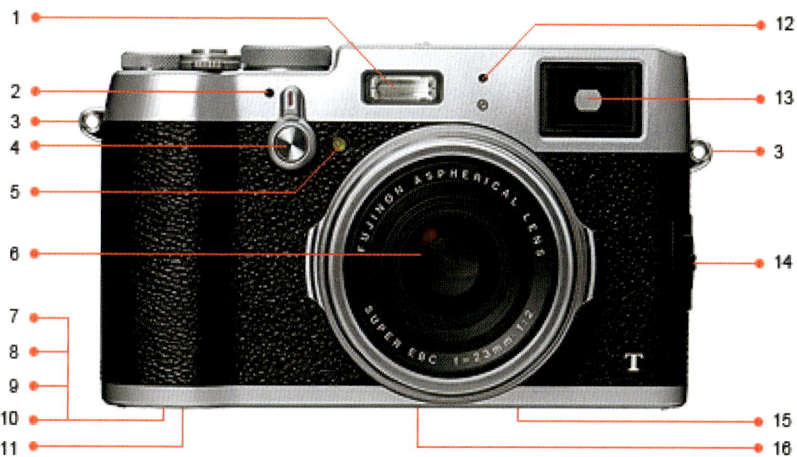

Figure 2.2: **Front view of the X100T**

1 Flash	9 Memory card slot
2 Microphone (right)	10 Battery chamber
3 Strap eyelet	11 Battery latch
4 Viewfinder selector	12 Microphone (left)
5 AF-assist illuminator	13 Viewfinder window
6 Lens	14 Focus mode selector
7 Battery cover	15 Speaker
8 Battery latch	16 Tripod mount

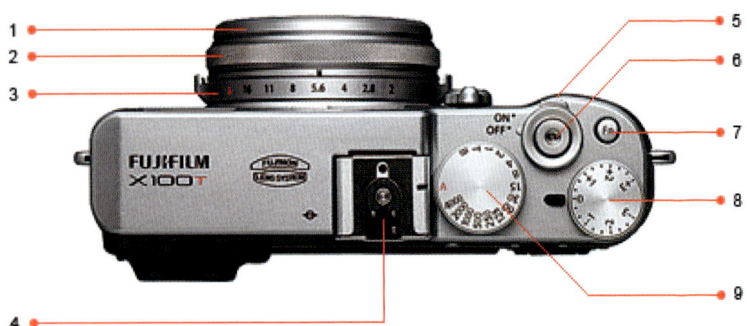

Figure 2.3: Top view of the X100T

1 Front ring
2 Focus ring
3 Aperture ring

4 Hot shoe
5 On/Off switch
6 Shutter button

7 Function button 1
8 Exposure compensation dial
9 Shutter speed dial

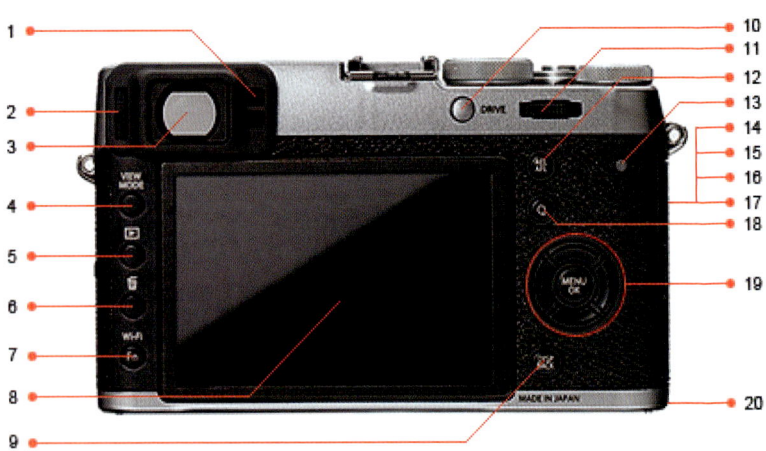

Figure 2.4: Rear view of the X100T

1 Eye sensor
2 Diopter adjustment
  control
3 Viewfinder window
4 View Mode button
5 Playback button
6 Delete button
  (function button 6)

7 Wi-Fi button
  (function button 7)
8 LCD monitor
9 Display/Back button
10 Drive button
11 Command dial
12 AEL/AFL button
13 Indicator lamp

14 Connector cover
15 Microphone/remote release
  connector
16 Micro USB connector
17 Micro HDMI connector
18 Q button
19 Selector (function buttons 2–4)
20 DC coupler cable cover

Here's where I admit that I belong to the group of people who consult instruction manuals only as a last resort because I prefer to learn by trial and error. This chapter is designed for people who want to pick up the essentials as quickly as possible before they start to photograph in earnest. Let's first take a look at the Setup menu for basic camera configurations. After you customize the settings, you'll primarily use the Quick menu (Q menu) and Shooting menu when taking pictures.

THE SHOOTING AND SETUP MENUS

The camera's classic design would quickly lose appeal if its operation weren't as elegant as its appearance. When people see the X100, they often exclaim, "Oh, that's a nice-looking retro model!" But labeling the X100 as a retro camera is much too limiting. It's no accident that manufacturers have been building 35mm cameras for decades with ergonomic controls that allow for intuitive operation. Fujifilm brought these same design principles into the digital world with the X100 series.

The X100 series does have menus that are specific to digital technology, but in contrast to many other camera systems I've used over the years, the menu structure of the Fujifilm X100 series is relatively clear and concise. (You can find a full overview of all the camera's programmable settings in the user manual [see chapter 5, "Links"].) In providing instructions for navigating the camera menus, I refer to Red 1 through Red 5 for the five main pages of the Shooting menu (figure 2.5), and Blue 1 through Blue 3 for the three main pages of the Setup menu. Submenus are indicated with an additional digit. This section addresses some particularly useful features.

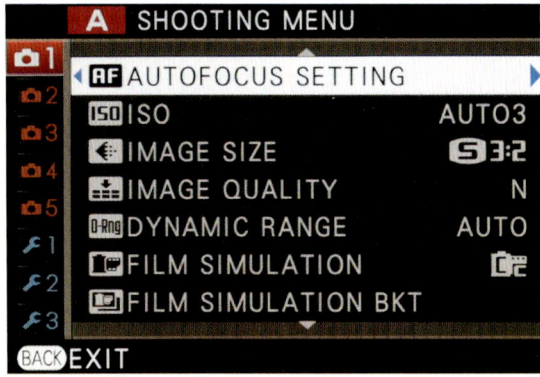

Figure 2.5: Shooting menu of the X100T

If you plan to focus manually, you'll find the Focus Check option (Blue 2.1) especially helpful. When this feature is activated, as soon as you adjust the focus ring the image will magnify in the display to make focusing easier. With focus peaking enabled (Red 3.7, MF Assist, Focus Peak Highlight), even difficult subjects pose no problem.

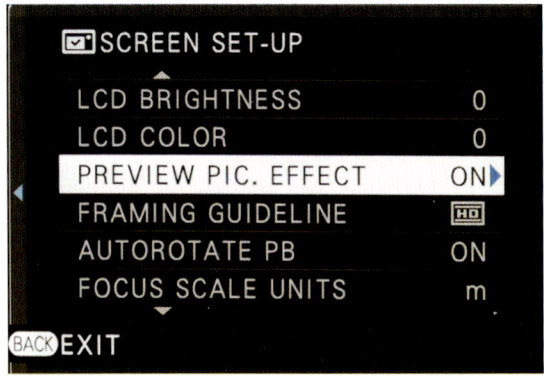

Figue 2.6 Previewing your exposure (Blue 2.3.9)

You can access the display settings at Blue 2.3. Here
you can turn Preview Exp. in Manual Mode on or off in
order to see a version of the image that either resembles
its final appearance based on the selected aperture, shutter speed, and ISO, or is a bright reproduction that is not
affected by these settings. In most cases, it's helpful to
preview the exposure settings and the image brightness,
but not always. For example, if you're shooting in a studio with flash and your ambient-light exposure settings
would usually result in an underexposed image (e.g.,
ISO 200, f/8, 1/180 second), the only way to examine the
focus is to disable this preview option.

X100T

With the Fujifilm X100T, you can automatically adjust the
brightness of the display in troublesome lighting conditions
(Blue 2.3.4), and you can switch off various image effects,
such as film simulations (Blue 2.3.9), so that you get a view
that is as close to reality as possible (natural live view mode).

X100S

The adjustment of the display in troublesome lighting conditions is set in the main menu (Blue 2.4.4), but all current
image settings are shown (WYSIWYG).

You can directly control the active AF field with the four
Selector buttons if you choose the Selector Button Setting
under Blue 2.4. You may decide, however, that giving up
four potential function buttons is too high a price.

Another helpful new feature is the ability to customize
the Q menu (Blue 2.5), both by reorganizing the order
of the items and removing less critical functions, such
as sharpness or color. It's best to sharpen your images
in dedicated editing software and with the end use for
your images in mind. Furthermore, you should work on a

calibrated monitor to adjust color, which is why I advise against making these adjustments in the camera. Removing those options from the Q menu would allow you, for example, to include the Conversion Lens feature on this menu, which enables you to quickly prep the camera for shooting with the wide-angle and teleconverter lenses.

NOTE

Sharpening images is a science unto itself, but I want to touch briefly on a few points. Sharpening your photographs is a key step in producing a brilliant, sharp image with great contrast, but your edits should always be tailored to your subject. For example, an atmospheric portrait and an architectural photograph will require different sharpness levels. Furthermore, the end use for your photos will demand different sharpening parameters. The key question is whether the image files will be edited and optimized on a computer or if they will be printed directly from the camera. In the former case, it's best to shoot RAW files and not sharpen images in the camera (set the sharpness to 0 or even −1); in the latter case, a modest amount of in-camera sharpening may make sense (set the sharpness to +1). The most common image editing programs have an abundance of sharpening functions and filters. The Unsharp Mask filter in Photoshop is one example. Sharpening amplifies the edge contrast. The extent to which the boundaries that separate bright and dark areas are accentuated can be controlled with the Amount slider. The Radius slider regulates how broadly the contrast adjustment is applied, and the Threshold slider determines how marked the contrast has to be for the sharpening effect to be applied. As a rule, a good starting range for Unsharp Mask parameters—again, depending on the end use for the photo—is to position the sliders as follows, in proportion to the image's final resolution: the Amount slider is set to about half of the pixels per inch (ppi), the Radius slider to 1/200 of the ppi, and the Threshold slider between 0 and 3 levels. For example, if you need to print an image at 300 ppi, start with settings of Amount 150%, Radius 1.5 pixels, and Threshold 0. If JPEG artifacts crop up during the sharpening process, carefully increase the Threshold setting. Sharpening should be the last step of your editing process, and it should be done only while viewing the image at 100%.

AUTO ISO

You can program the Auto ISO settings by navigating to the Red 1.2 menu, where you can set the default sensitivity, the maximum sensitivity, and the minimum shutter speed. To prevent camera shake, for example, you might set the minimum shutter speed to 1/60 second.

X100T

The Fujifilm X100T allows you to program three Auto ISO profiles, which you can quickly access via the Q menu based on the shooting circumstances.

THE NEUTRAL DENSITY (ND) FILTER

The Fujifilm X100 cameras feature an integrated ND filter (Red 2.1), which effectively reduces the exposure by three stops. This tool is especially useful in bright, backlit situations when you want to shoot with a wide aperture. Use the built-in Noise Reduction (Red 2.6) technology with caution because it tends to produce unsightly artifacts. I recommend sticking to values in the −1 to 0 range. The X-Trans sensor does a fantastic job of rendering image noise—or digital grain, as I prefer to call it. Even in difficult lighting, distracting digital noise is not detectable when using ISO settings from 200 to 6400, although you should test this yourself by shooting a bracketed sequence. For long-exposure images it's worthwhile to edit the RAF file with a dedicated noise-reduction software, such as Imagenomic Noiseware, instead of relying on the camera's internal system (Red 2.7, Long Exposure NR). Menu Red 3.6 is important for adjusting the viewfinder when you use the wide-angle or teleconverter lens. Consider adding this setting to the fully customizable Q menu.

Focus peaking and the more traditional digital split-image indicator can both be configured under MF Assist (Red 3.7). Section 2.3, "In Focus," goes into greater detail about these methods.

ELECTRONIC SHUTTER

X100T

Fujifilm equipped the X100T with a new digital shutter that is capable of shutter speeds between 1/4000 and 1/32,000 second.

Users can select one of three shutter options (Red 5.5, Shutter Type): the mechanical shutter (MS), which can produce shutter speeds from 1/4000 second to 30 seconds (set by adjusting the shutter speed dial); the electronic shutter (ES); or a combination of the two (MS+ES). It may be desirable to use the electronic shutter for slower shutter speeds when you don't want shutter noise, but the primary application for the electronic shutter is shooting with a wide aperture in bright backlit situations.

On such occasions, an ND filter (also known as a gray filter) may also be used. These filters are made of optical glass or plastic, and they darken an image without distorting the colors. An ND filter's effective strength, or the degree to which it reduces the light that reaches the sensor, is often indicated by optical density, or NDx. The camera's internal ND filter, which can be switched on or off, has an effective optical density of NDx = 0.9, which means that 12.6% of the light is transmitted, the shutter speed is effectively increased by a factor of eight, and the exposure is reduced by three stops. The strength of this filter isn't sufficient for very powerfully bright sunlight, which might require an NDx = 3.0 filter (with 0.1% transmittance, an effective shutter speed elongation factor of 1,000, and an effective 10-stop reduction of the exposure). Without a filter, you might opt to shoot with shutter speeds of 1/800, 1/16,000, or 1/32,000 second to reduce the amount of light in your exposure. But if you think you'll be able to freeze speeding bullets in your photos, even at those fast shutter speeds you'll be disappointed.

Objects that move very quickly suffer from the "rolling shutter effect," which produces artifacts that result from the line-by-line scanning mechanism of a CMOS sensor. Objects that move very quickly may change position from one line to the next. The resulting image does not portray a static object, but rather an interpolation of the object at different moments in time. Using the electronic shutter also precludes the possibility of shooting with flash.

FILE NAMES

People who like to stay organized will appreciate the Edit File Name function in the Setup menu (Blue 3.1). The two available color spaces—sRGB and Adobe RGB—can be saved with different file name structures. Photographers who use multiple cameras might take advantage of this feature to code their photos based on which camera was used. This function is especially helpful when photographing events because there is often need to make images available as soon as possible. Instead of using the default file name convention, you could use an abbreviated form of your name. For sRGB exposures there are four alphanumeric characters that precede the continuous numbering (e.g., *FA00*1234.jpg); for Adobe RGB images there are only three leading characters because the first character is fixed (e.g., *_FA0*1234.jpg).

THE Q MENU

James Bond fans know Q as the research and development mastermind who equips Bond with gadgets to stay one step ahead of his nemeses. For Fujifilm X-Series photographers, the Q menu is a quick and elegant solution for adjusting key shooting settings, such as ISO, white balance, file format, film simulation, and many more, without having to navigate deep into the camera menus. This menu of shortcuts makes it easy to get started with the camera and avoids the inevitable frustration that ensues when you sift through countless menus to find a setting. Even experienced photographers will appreciate the convenience of accessing camera features quickly.

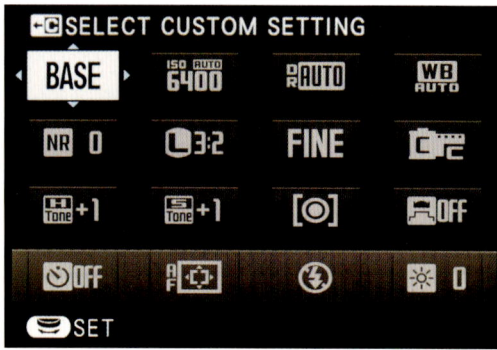

Figure 2.7: The Q menu on the X100T

X100T

The X100T offers a fully customizable Q menu that allows users to specify which functions are included in it and their order on the menu. Set up the menu to accommodate your own personal preferences.

To customize the Q menu, select Edit/Save Quick Menu from the Setup menu (Blue 2.5). The first page of the factory settings for the Q menu gives you access to ISO value, dynamic range, white balance, noise reduction, image size, image quality, film simulation, highlight tone, shadow tone, color saturation, and sharpness. If you navigate past the first screen, you can control the self-timer, the AF mode, the flash mode, and the brightness of the display. Use the Selector buttons to navigate through the Q menu, and use the command dial to change the highlighted setting. There is no need to confirm your selection; just press the shutter button and the camera will be ready to shoot with the new settings. To bring up the configuration menu, press and hold the Q button.

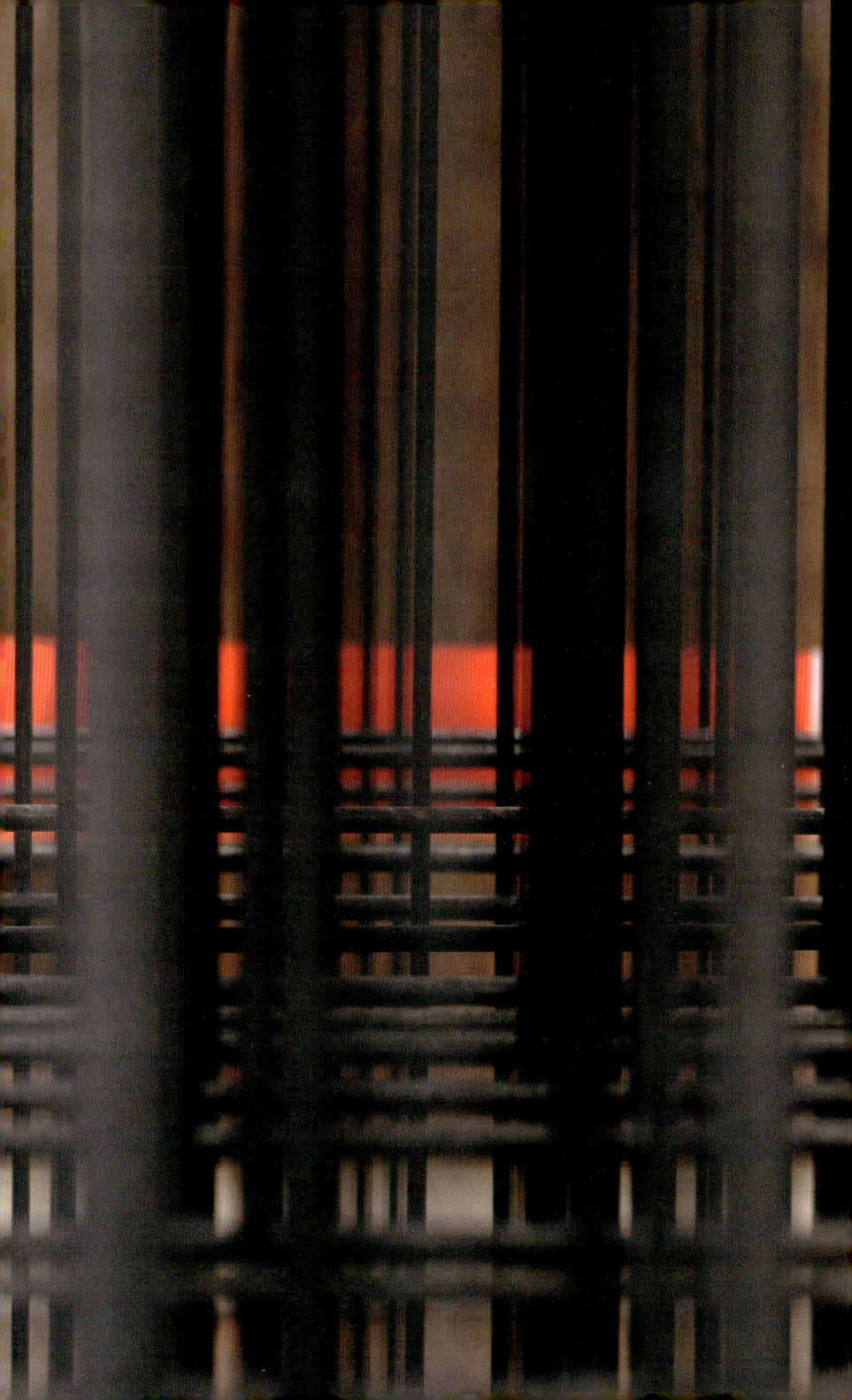

2.2 Exposure Control

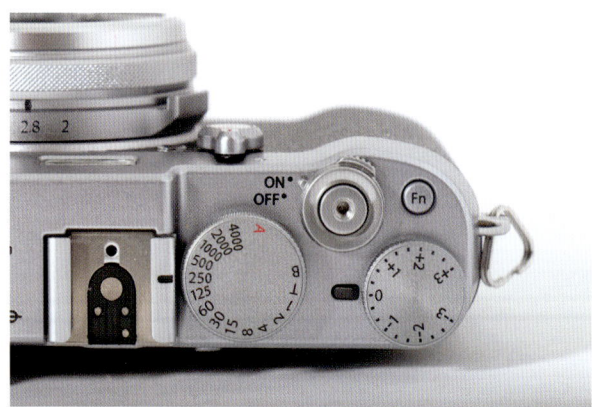

Figure 2.8: **Top view of the camera**

The aperture ring and shutter speed dial make it easy to set these two key exposure parameters. Use the Q menu to set your desired ISO value or the acceptable range of values if you're using an Auto ISO option.

X100T

You can use the exposure compensation dial on the top right of the camera to adjust the exposure by three stops up or down—even in manual exposure mode, as long as Auto ISO is enabled.

The aperture priority, shutter priority, and manual exposure modes will be familiar to DSLR photographers. In these semiautomatic modes, you choose either the aperture or the shutter speed, and the camera automatically chooses the other setting. Activate these modes by selecting A on the aperture ring or the shutter speed dial.

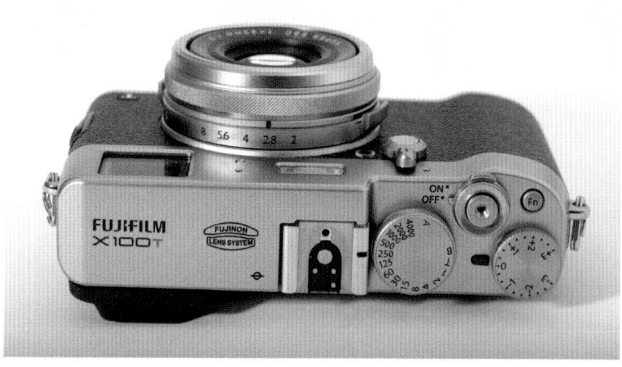

Figure 2.9: Using the aperture ring of the X100T to set the aperture. Here it is set to f/2.8.

Keep in mind that you must set a specific ISO value or set the camera to Auto ISO so it can choose a value. Remember that when you use an automatic or semiautomatic exposure mode, the camera attempts to coordinate the shutter speed, aperture, and ISO settings to achieve an overall neutral gray exposure with 18% reflectance in the ambient shooting conditions. You might assume this means you will always get balanced exposures that are not too bright or too dark, but that is not the case.

An 18% reflectance of the ambient light corresponds to the center of Zone V in the 11-zone system developed by Ansel Adams. Image areas with a maximum brightness of 100% (pure white) correspond to Zone X. As you go down the scale, the intensity of each zone decreases (by a factor of 1 divided by the square root of 2). Zone 0 corresponds to 3.13% light intensity, essentially pure black. The camera's exposure meter is calibrated to assume that appealing images feature an average distribution of tonal values, so it determines an integral value for that distribution. But not all scenes have an "average distribution of tonal values." Therefore, the exposure for some predominantly dark or light subjects needs to be adjusted if the image is to correspond to the actual brightness of the subject. To illustrate this point, imagine a wedding taking place high up in the mountains. The bride is standing on snow, so the image will need to be overexposed to depict the snow and white wedding dress with their true brilliance (the entire subject is significantly lighter than neutral gray). Conversely, for another shot the groom is standing in a dark area of a mountain lodge, so the image needs to be underexposed because the camera's attempt to achieve an average of neutral gray will result in a picture that is too bright. This is where the exposure compensation dial can help.

As with many cameras on the market today, the Fujifilm X100T and X100S offer three metering modes: multi, spot, and average. Multi metering attempts to optimize the exposure by automatically recognizing the subject; this is the best metering method for most shooting situations. Spot metering uses the light values in the selected focus area or in the center of the frame to determine the exposure. When you shoot a subject that has a significant difference in brightness from the background—a portrait in front of a bright background, for example—spot metering is often the best way to correctly expose the subject. In this situation, average metering would produce an underexposed subject because it calculates an average brightness for the entire frame. Average metering is a practical approach for capturing balanced, neutral exposures of subjects like landscapes.

If you want to change the metering method on the fly, either configure the Q menu to include Photometry or assign the capability to one of the seven programmable function (Fn) buttons.

HIGH ISO

The powerful combination of the high-quality image sensor and the EXR Processor II means you can capture low-noise images with ISO settings ranging from 200 to 6400 (and with usable results up to ISO 51,200). The Auto ISO feature that many photographers favor allows you to save three profiles that you can set up for different shooting situations. The Auto ISO profiles allow you to define the standard sensitivity (ISO 200 is a good choice), the highest allowable sensitivity (up to ISO 6400), and a minimum shutter speed threshold to ensure that exposures are free from camera shake. When you shoot RAW files, ISO values from 200 to 6400 are available; you can select higher or lower values only when you shoot JPEGs. Higher ISO sensitivities are made possible through internal adjustments to the tone curve and other image optimization parameters.

THE "CORRECT" EXPOSURE

At this point, you may be wondering what a correct exposure is and how to achieve it. The common approaches that photographers take in order create a "good" exposure are 1) capturing the standard (or "correct") exposure, 2) underexposing modestly, and 3) exposing to the right. "Exposing to the right" means forcing the histogram, which portrays a distribution of tonal values from dark (left) to bright (right), to shift as far as possible to the brightest possible values that still hold detail. I'll discuss that more later, but first let's look at a few underlying issues to understand when using these exposure techniques.

There are three key characteristics of digital photographs that will inform your choice. First, darker tonal values are more likely to suffer from noticeable image noise. Second, it becomes impossible to distinguish among light tonal values above a certain threshold; after that, everything looks like pure white (RGB values of 255, 255, 255)—this is called "clipped" or "blown-out" highlights, or the pure white areas of an image that have no detail. Third, scenes may not contain all the values within the camera's full dynamic range; as a result, some tonal values are not represented in the image. (A related fact is that digital sensors are inferior to the human eye when it comes to perceiving dark tonal values.)

The key to creating a good exposure is to work within the limitations of the camera's sensor while exploiting its strengths. To create an ideal exposure, you would capture a standard exposure that encompasses the full range of tonal values in the scene, from dark to light, with no clipping in the darkest or lightest parts of the image. The shadows and highlights would still have detail, or discernible visual information. This is not possible in practical, "real-world" terms because it's impossible to know the exact distribution of tonal values in a scene before you release the shutter, and shooting a second photo with adjusted exposure settings is not always an option. Furthermore, some scenes exhibit a range of tonal values that is actually broader than the camera's sensor can capture.

Given these constraints, you need a plan to capture an optimal exposure. Let's consider the first strategy: capturing a correct exposure that requires no adjustments during post-processing. In this approach, the midlevel gray tones in the subject should correspond to middle gray on the histogram. The average metering method lends itself nicely to this purpose, and you should avoid clipping the shadows and highlights if possible. When you use average metering, the target brightness is immediately apparent, and you can evaluate the exposure on the camera display. This method eliminates the need for extensive post-processing. One of the dangers of this method, however, is the risk of clipping the highlights, especially for images that have a lot of contrast (i.e., when the scene has both very bright and very dark tones).

The second exposure strategy, underexposing images by fractions of a stop, is a holdover from the days of shooting with slide film, and it was used to enhance contrast in the image. To use this method with your X100, use the multi

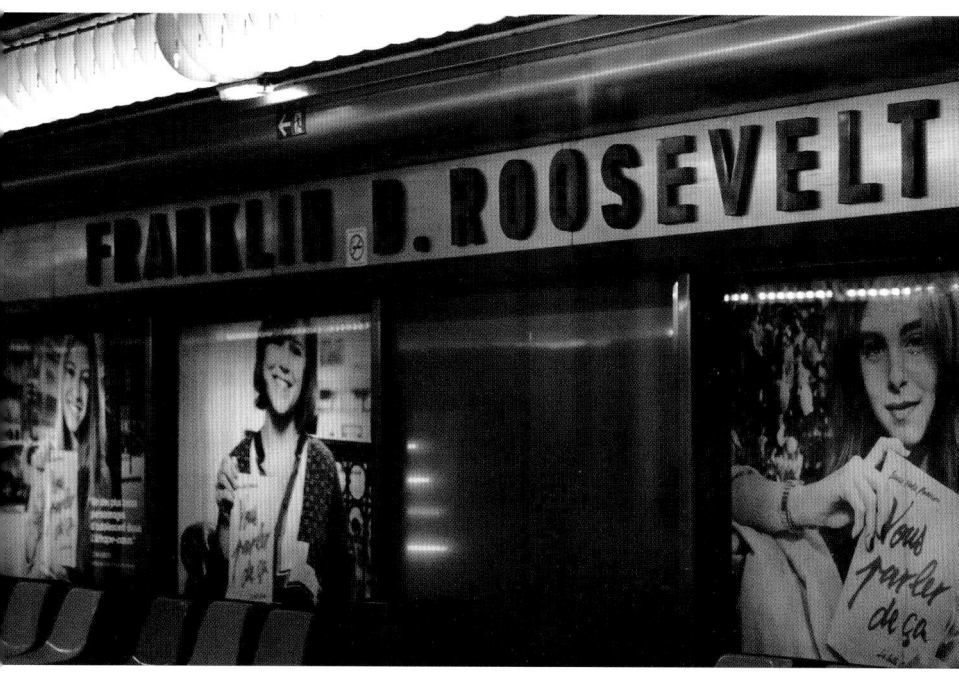

metering method and adjust the exposure compensation dial to reduce the exposure by 1/3 or 2/3 stop. Depending on the scene and your objectives, you can carefully increase the exposure during post-processing. You need to shoot in RAW mode (or RAW+JPEG) to get the maximum image quality. The advantage of this method is that you reduce the risk of clipping the highlights. The disadvantage is that your images are more susceptible to problematic image noise when you brighten the darker areas during post-processing. If you tend to check the exposure on the camera monitor, you'll have to make an allowance for the intended under-exposure. This approach yields a modest reduction in the number of tonal values of an image.

The third strategy, exposing to the right of the histogram, is the most difficult. The goal is to expose your images with the tonal values mapped as far to the right of the histogram as possible without clipping any of the highlights. A logical way to achieve this is to use spot metering on the brightest part of the scene, then use the exposure compensation dial to make adjustments. Most of the time this technique will result in an overexposed picture, but you can bring the image back to a normal exposure by lowering the overall exposure values of the RAW file during post-processing. The benefit of this approach is that it maximizes the number of captured tonal values while minimizing image noise. Because you end up with brighter tonal values in the image (compared to a standard exposure), there is less noise in the image after you darken it. The extent to which noise is reduced depends on how much you can overexpose the image without losing detail in the highlights. The risk of using this method is that you can shift the histogram too far to the right and suffer a loss of image data, particularly in the individual color channels, which can result in unnatural color shifts. It takes some practice to evaluate the live image with this technique because the JPEG preview of the RAW data will look overexposed. Some people argue that this method requires photographers to shoot several test pictures to collect the needed information so they can position the histogram in the targeted area. The counterargument is that the live histogram function on the X100T gives you the power to evaluate the tonal values in the viewfinder or on the camera display before you release the shutter.

NOTE

The benefits of exposing to the right become clearer when you consider how digital sensors process light signals. Sensors have a matrix of photodiodes that produce an electric charge proportional in voltage to the amount of incident light received. The diodes' range of sensitivity (from the minimum quantity of light they can detect to the maximum overflow quantity) is what defines the dynamic range of the sensor—or, in terms of the image, the range between the darkest areas (shadows) and brightest areas (highlights) that still exhibit discernible detail. ▶

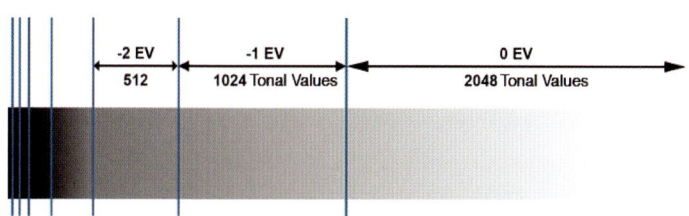

Figure 2.10: For a dynamic range of eight exposure values (EV), exactly 50% of the tonal values are for the brightness levels between 87.5% and 100%. In contrast, less than 1% of the tonal values are available for the brightness levels between 0% and 12.5%. © Martin Vieten

The conversion of a brightness level to a voltage value is linear. Technically speaking, the digital tone curve is exactly diagonal, whereas the curve for film can exhibit a soft or hard gradation. For digital sensors, this characteristic means that each brightness value corresponds to a specific voltage value, and voltage values are evenly spaced.

A downstream analog-to-digital converter translates the voltage value into a digital quantity. There are 4,096 tonal values for a standard image size of 12 bits. For a dynamic range of 8 EV, there is a varying number of tonal values available for each stop, as illustrated in table 2.1.

Exposure Values	Tonal Values
0 EV	2048
−1 EV	1024
−2 EV	512
−3 EV	256
−4 EV	128
−5 EV	64
−6 EV	32
−7 EV	16

Table 2.1: Tonal values as a function of exposure values

Table 2.1 shows that the brightest areas of the image have 2,048 tonal values available, while only 16 tonal values are available for the darkest areas. Producing rich detail for the darkest areas of the image is just not possible. However, shifting the distribution to the brighter exposure values increases the number of tonal values in the image file. You can then darken the exposure in a RAW converter during post-processing.

Some scenes may tolerate a loss of detail in the highlights without any problems. Allowing bright spots—such as reflections of sunlight on water or metal, or lamps and other light sources—to clip a little won't be a problem in many images. If you expose a typical sunset so no highlight areas are clipped, you'll end up with a vastly underexposed foreground. In other cases, you may have to lose some detail, even if you'd rather not. The trick is to figure out how much clipping to allow without ruining the overall look and feel you want in your image. Remember that blown-out highlights, especially when individual color channels are lost, can result in undesirable color shifts.

In summary, the best exposure technique and metering method depends on the subject. Having a clear understanding of the factors that influence exposure helps you decide whether clipped highlights or some image noise are acceptable. No matter what approach you take, it is always best to shoot in RAW mode when the contrast in a scene exceeds the sensor's dynamic range or if you expose to the right, despite the fact that Fujifilm is known for high-quality JPEGs. RAW files allow more flexibility in post-processing so you don't have to sacrifice quality. If a subject has a relatively modest contrast range and there aren't any bright light sources or reflections in the scene, you can stick with capturing the standard exposure. Underexposure almost always leads to a loss of detail in the shadows. When you shoot subjects with a wide contrast range, it's safe to say that shifting the histogram toward the highlights is generally the best approach.

EXPOSURE BRACKETING

A quick way to find the optimal exposure with the X100T and X100S is to use the automatic exposure bracketing function (AE BKT). When this feature is activated, the camera takes three pictures each time you press the shutter button: one at the baseline exposure, one overexposed

by a predetermined amount, and one underexposed by
the same predetermined amount. Because of the time
lapse between exposures, AE BKT is best suited for stationary or slow-moving subjects. When you expose an image
to the right of the histogram, it's most effective to use
small exposure increments (e.g.,–1/3, 0, +1/3) to produce
the brightest possible exposure that is not clipped, but
larger increments (e.g.,–2, 0, +2) can be used for subjects
that have a large contrast range. During post-processing
you can use high dynamic range (HDR) editing software
to combine the three bracketed images into one final photograph. For example, if you shoot an interior scene during
the day in a room with windows, a correct exposure of
the interior elements (such as a dark leather sofa and
wood floors) will cause outdoor elements that are visible
through the window to be washed out; conversely, if you
expose for the bright outdoor elements (a sky with white
clouds, perhaps), all the detail in the interior elements
will be lost. The range of contrast in the scene exceeds
what the sensor can capture in one exposure. However, if
you bracket three images, with the exposures set for the
shadows, the middle tones, and the highlights, you can
create an HDR photograph that reveals rich levels of detail
in all areas, resulting in a natural overall appearance.

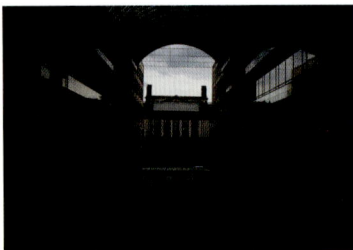

Figure 2.11.1: 1/1000 second

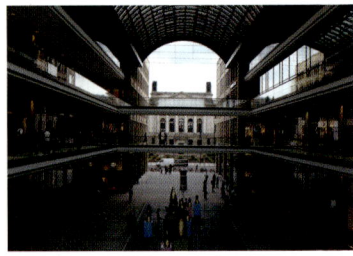

Figure 2.11.2: 1/250 second

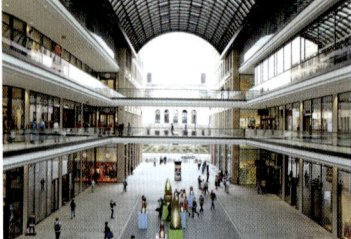

Figure 2.11.3: 1/60 second

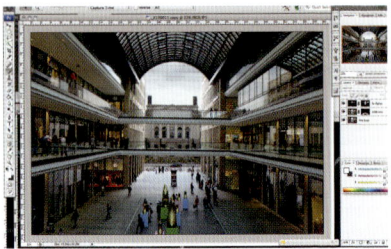

Figure 2.11.4: Photoshop layers

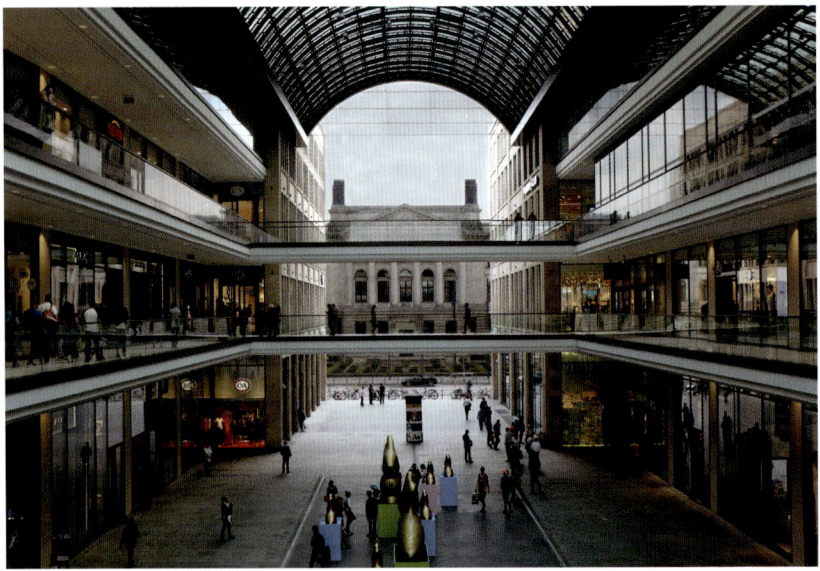

Figure 2.11.5: Final HDR image, with component images (2.11.1, 2.11.2, and 2.11.3) and Photoshop screenshot (2.11.4)

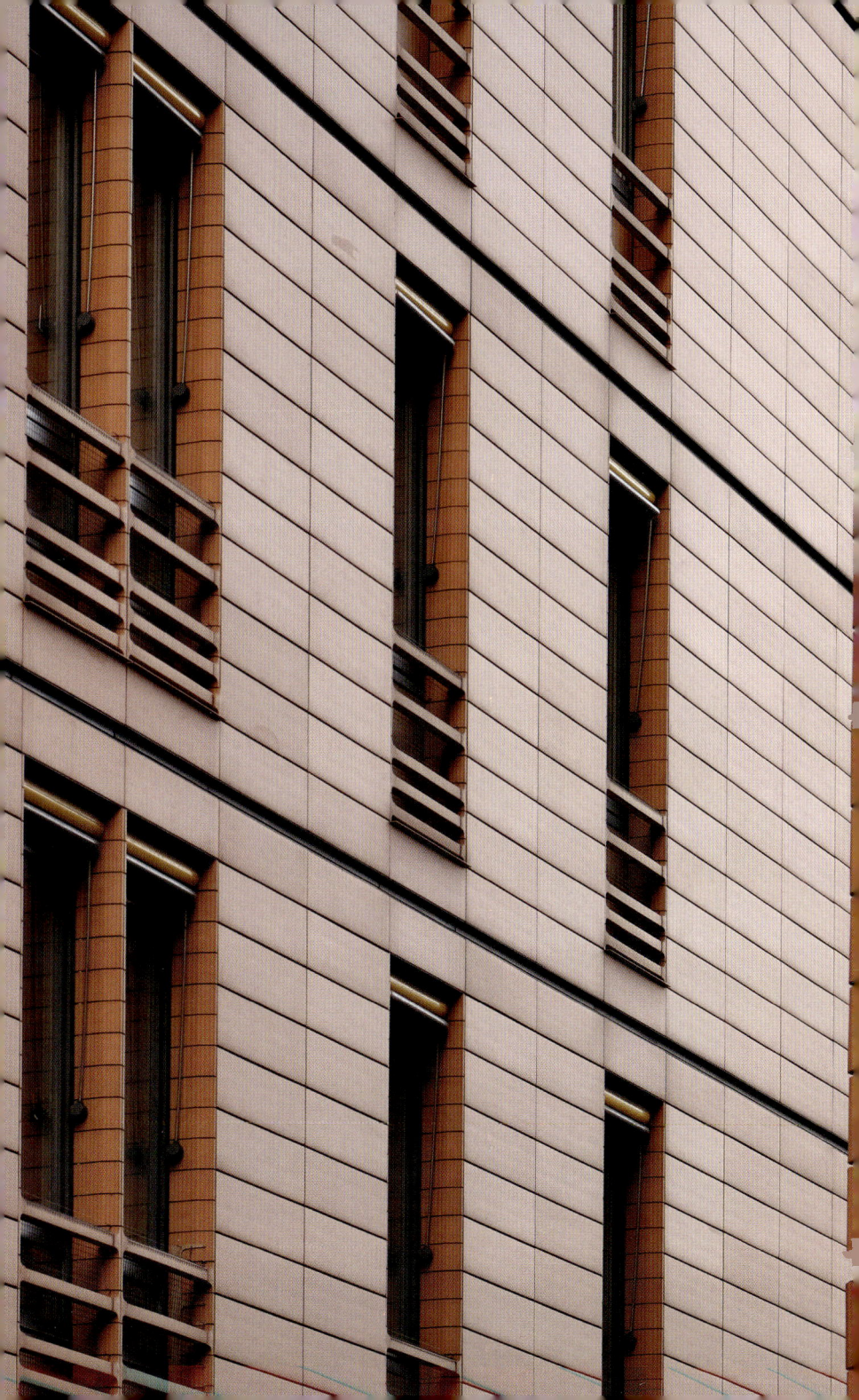

2.3 In Focus

As with the Fujifilm X100S, the focus mode selector on the side of the X100T has three options: manual (M), continuous (C), and single (S).

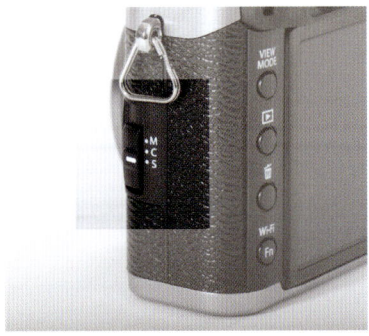

Figure 2.12: **Focus mode selector**

Let's first take a closer look at the different types of auto-focus (AF) techniques. Specifically, let's look at Contrast Detection AF (CDAF) and Phase Detection AF (PDAF). CDAF measures contrast by comparing micro contrast differences between neighboring sensor pixels. Its aim is to achieve the highest contrast between pixels, which indicates that the image is in focus. In order to find this maximum amount of contrast, several measurements are necessary. As there is no distance measurement involved, CDAF is critical when it comes to tracking moving subjects. On the plus side, CDAF is more precise compared to PDAF, where the incoming light is split into two images and then compared. When those two images match, focus has been achieved. In all other cases, the phase shift is used in order to calculate the movement of lens elements via AF motors to achieve a sharp and in-focus image. This technique requires only one measurement, which makes it quick and appropriate for tracking focus on fast-moving objects. To summarize, it's accurate to say that CDAF is continuously adjusting focus until maximum contrast (and therefore sharpness) is reached, while PDAF determines the optimal focus position in one attempt. Combining both methods results in the Hybrid AF of the X100T, which switches between the very fast PDAF and the highly precise CDAF, depending on the subject and shooting situation. This also allows for fast and reliable focusing in poor lighting conditions.

NOTE

On both the X100T and X100S, the Phase Detection pixels are only located in the center area (the inner 3 × 3 AF fields).

The single AF (AF-S) mode is primarily for focusing on stationary or slowly moving subjects, such as landscapes, buildings, and people who are posing for portraits. For both the X100T and X100S, one can set the active AF frame to any of the 49 AF positions by pressing the Selector buttons or using a fixed AF field (preferably the center one), establishing the focus by pressing the shutter button halfway, then reorienting the camera to compose the image. After you press the shutter button completely, the focus will remain on the originally targeted subject. This is a quick process that allows for precise focusing and maximum sharpness. It is important to adjust the size of the active AF field with the command dial in order to optimize the AF performance. As a general rule, the AF field should be set as large as possible and as small as necessary in order to target the surface of the subject that should be in focus. If the size of the AF field matches the size of the subject, one obtains optimal performance. Taking a close-up shot of a small structure would be a case where reducing the AF field size is strongly recommended. Many DSLR shooters still have a "Let's focus on the edge between the subject and the background" approach in mind—this is not the right approach when using CDAF.

The AF speed is, generally speaking, faster with a larger AF field, but when focusing on a small structure (like a specific detail of a small object or one eye in a close-up portrait), it is recommended that you gradually reduce the size of the AF field.

The Face Detection feature (Red 1.1.6) added to the X100T is useful when you photograph people in motion. It automatically positions the AF field on a face. As long as the person is more or less looking at the camera, face detection is remarkably accurate. If the camera doesn't detect a face within the image area, the autofocus system proceeds with its normal operation.

When you are shooting a moving subject, or if you are moving toward the subject, continuous autofocus (AF-C) is always the best choice—one might think. When it is active, the camera tries to adjust the focus for every detectable motion. You can pair AF-C with burst shooting mode, which captures either three (continuous low, CL) or six (continuous high, CH) images per second for both camera models, then you can choose the best result. The effectiveness of this approach, and continuous autofocus in general, depends on the lighting conditions and how fast the subject or you are moving. One general difference between the X100S and X100T is that the former operates with AF priority, which means it's not willing to release the shutter and take the shot until focus is locked or it "gives up," which means most likely a wasted shot.

X100S

Generally speaking, it's advisable to distinguish between subjects that are far away and subjects that are nearby. In the first scenario, when AF-C is used one can opt for a slower or faster burst rate (CL versus CH), stop down the lens in order to have a sufficient depth of field (e.g., f/5.6 or higher) and choose a fast enough shutter speed (e.g., 1/250 second or faster) in order to freeze the movement. It should be mentioned that even if only one ▶

cross is visible in the center of the screen, the inner 3 × 3 focusing fields are also in use. For near subjects, the number of in-focus images will increase when selecting AF-S combined with a slower or faster burst rate (drive modes CL or CH), again with the appropriate f-stop values for a sufficient depth of field and a fast enough shutter speed. Using back-button autofocus instead of the widely used "half-pressing the shutter" technique is worth trying. One should press the shutter button all the way through in one motion.

The X100T offers a more sophisticated way of handling focus in situations with subjects in motion. Inside shooting menu Red 1.3, there is an option to select between Focus Priority or Release Priority for both AF-S and AF-C modes. Let's look at a couple different scenarios. Imagine shooting racecars on a track where you are at quite a distance from the cars. Selecting Release Priority and AF-C mode (shooting at continuous high drive mode) will yield a higher number of shots per burst compared to using Focus Priority mode. In Release Priority, the image is captured even if it's not perfectly in focus. Taking the depth of field at a chosen aperture (e.g., f/8) and the distance from you to the subject (e.g., 70 feet) into account, this setup will, nevertheless, result in a large number of in-focus frames. By contrast, imagine a scenario where you are taking pictures of a child on a playground running towards a proud parent—this scenario would suggest selecting Focus Priority mode and AF-C, combined with continuous low or high drive mode. The obligatory condition—the shot has to be in focus— might slightly reduce the burst speed, but it increases the number of in-focus shots.

You should know that, if you're using either continuous drive mode (CL or CH), when you use continuous autofocus (AF-C) each single frame is focused. But if you are using single frame autofocus (AF-S), only the first frame is focused and the following images are not refocused.

X100T

Multiple target auto area AF, which uses multiple AF fields to focus on a subject, is a new feature in the Fujifilm X100T. This feature considerably increases the AF performance and hit rate (Menu Red 1.5, AF Mode Multi) when used in AF-C mode.

Combining this feature with continuous focusing is an effective way to track moving subjects. However, if the main subject is surrounded by a busy, contrasty background, the autofocus may zero in on the wrong part of the image area. In these situations, it's easier to use a fixed AF frame or to use continuous focusing with the central AF frame (Menu Red 1.5, AF Mode Area). For both the X100S and X100T, the Power Management option "high performance mode" should be activated (X100S: Blue 2.5.2; X100T: Blue 2.6.3). A little higher energy consumption rate is well worth the gain in autofocus speed.

MANUAL FOCUSING

Most improvements to the focusing capabilities of the X100T apply to manual focusing. As with previous models, you slide the focus mode selector on the side of the camera to M, for manual focusing. The focus ring on the lens makes it easy to focus with precision and speed.

The focus ring is not physically connected to the focus control on the lens; instead, it operates with focus-by-wire technology, which sends electronic commands to the control. This technology correlates the speed of focusing with how fast you turn the ring, which makes it easy to quickly move the focus back and forth between near and far objects.

As with all cameras in the Fujifilm X-Series, you can always press the AEL/AFL button to engage autofocus. Many photographers do this first to get a ballpark focus, then they make minor adjustments with the focus ring.

There are three ways to evaluate sharpness while you manually focus. First, you can consult the distance scale along the bottom edge of the optical and electronic viewfinder windows and on the LCD monitor.

X100T

The white indicator on the scale reveals the distance to the object that is currently in focus, and the blue indicator corresponds to the current depth of field.

X100S

The red indicator on the scale reveals the distance to the object that is currently in focus, and the white indicator corresponds to the current depth of field.

This feature is convenient for selecting the correct aperture for the desired depth of field. When you change the aperture, the depth of field indicator automatically updates. When you press the center of the command dial, the focus area is magnified so you can fine-tune the focus. The magnification factor for the focus check window is adjustable.

Second, you can activate Digital Split Image in the Setup menu (Red 3.7, MF Assist, for both the X100T and the X100S) to evaluate manual focus. This tool harkens back to the classic split-image indicators from the days of film. When the elements in the focusing frame are aligned (especially horizontal details), the focus is set.

FOCUS PEAKING

Focus peaking (located at Red 3.7, MF Assist, for both the X100T and the X100S) is the third way to control manual focus. It highlights edges and contours of objects that are in focus with high contrast. This is my favorite way to adjust manual focus, in part because it provides useful depth-of-field information in real time. Depth-of-field preview, a comparable feature in some DSLRs, is sometimes problematic because the viewfinder image can get dark when using medium and small aperture openings. The focus peak highlighting makes it easy to evaluate which elements are within the current depth of field so you can adjust the aperture as needed. As an improvement compared to the X100S, there are now two intensities of three colors (white, red, and blue) to choose from. Experiment with three objects arranged diagonally on a table to discover the benefits of this feature.

X100T

The widely praised electronic rangefinder displays a small version of the electronic viewfinder in the lower-right corner of the optical viewfinder. Both the split-image indicator and focus peaking are available with this feature.

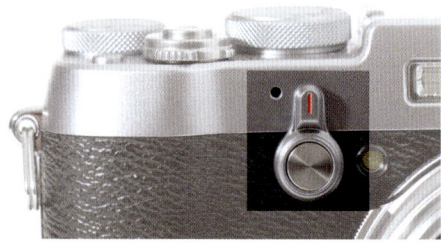

Figure 2.13: The viewfinder selector on the front of the camera

At first glance, the variety of manual focus tools may seem overwhelming, but you'll quickly discover your favorites and learn that specific shooting situations lend themselves to a particular method. When it is critical to evaluate the ambient lighting conditions, many photographers find that the zoomed focus check with the parallax-corrected optical viewfinder is the best way to adjust manual focus. The optical viewfinder allows very precise work because it displays a window that is actually larger than the image area. Many other viewfinders display a window that is smaller

than the image area (around 95% to 98%), which sometimes makes it necessary to crop out distracting elements
that you may not have been able to see in the viewfinder,
but they are visible when the image is viewed at 100%. The
electronic viewfinder in the X100T shows the exact capture
area and the exposure that corresponds to the current settings (Blue 2.3.3). It can be useful to preview the exposure in
low-light situations or at night so you can decide if exposure
compensation is needed. With the three-inch LCD monitor
and the focus check zoom feature, which is activated when
you press the center of the command dial, you always have a
quick and effective way to inspect the focus.

MACRO PHOTOS

The X100T and X100S are more than adequate for photo-
graphically exploring the world of the miniature, but serious
macro photography requires a true macro lens. If you want
to try your hand at macro photography with the X100T,
experiment a bit and test the limits of its performance.

Figures 2.14–2.17 show an ornament that was photographed at the minimum focal distance of the lens with
autofocus. No external light sources or reflectors were
used to capture these photos.

Figure 2.14: Macro
photo, f/2, 1/60 second,
ISO 640

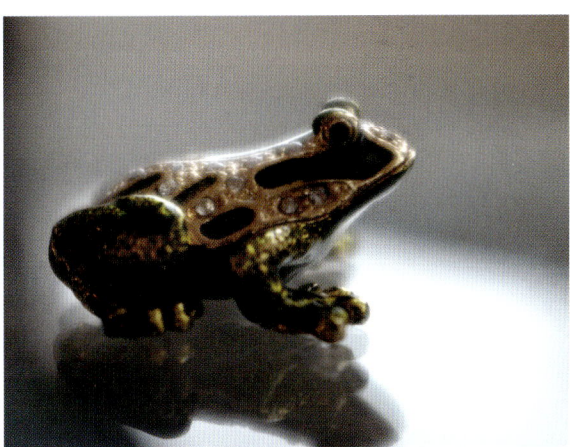

These photos were shot without a tripod at a subject distance of roughly four inches. Figure 2.14 reveals some areas of modest blur. Shooting under the identical circumstances and adding the built-in flash (reduced to −2) produced a photo that is colorful, brilliant, and rich in contrast (figure 2.15).

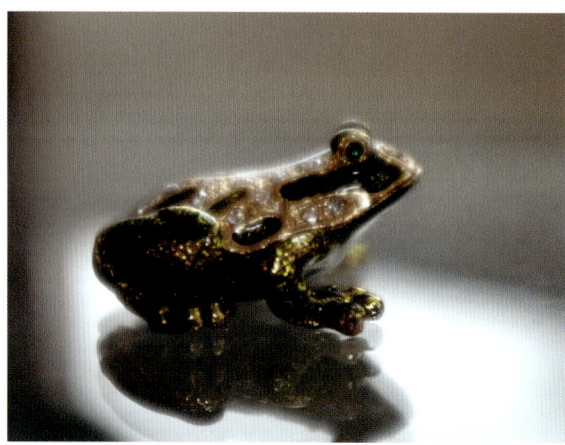

Figure 2.15: Macro photo, f/2, 1/60 second, ISO 500, flash −2

The wide-open aperture causes the subject to stand out nicely against a blurred background. Stopping down slightly produces an image that is high enough quality for a product catalog because the jewel details are clear (figure 2.16).

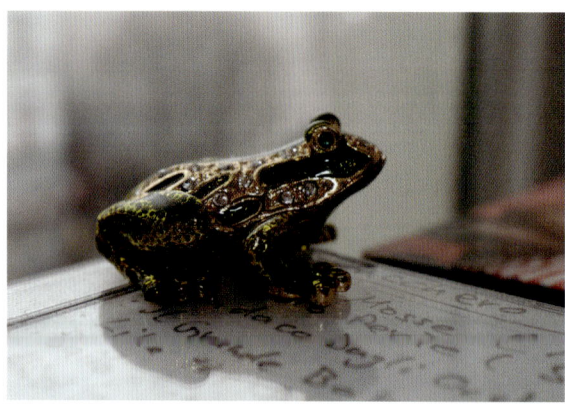

Figure 2.16: Macro photo, f/5.6, 1/30 second, ISO 640, flash −2

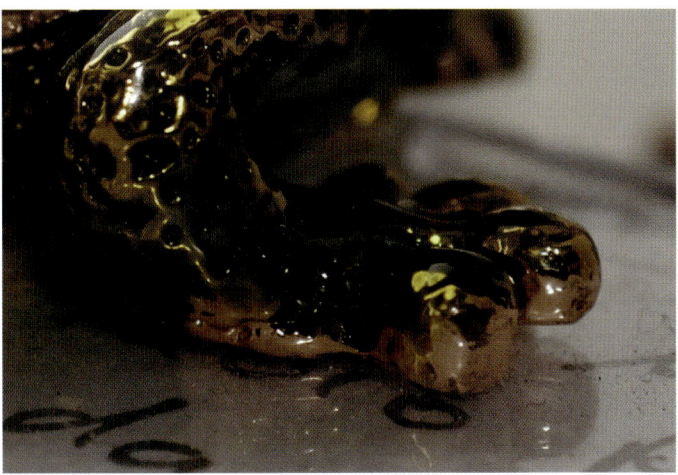

Figure 2.17: 100% view of figure 2.16 image detail

Don't leave the lens hood (or even some filters) attached to the lens when you shoot macro photos; if the flash fires, they may cast unsightly shadows on the subject. The X100T and X100S have more than enough macro muscle to tackle macro images for online use, such as for sales and marketing. With a little more effort—using a small table-top tripod, making an attractive backdrop (e.g., inserting a sheet of paper into a small infinity cove), and using an additional light source or reflector—you can take professional-grade product photos of small objects.

In shooting situations that put autofocus to the test, activate High Performance mode, which is on the Setup menu (Blue 2.6.3). It will drain the battery faster, but the autofocus will track moving objects better and faster. If you want to power up the camera quickly, deactivate the OVF Power Save Mode (Blue 2.6.2).

2.4 Image Quality, Image Size, and the X-Trans Sensor

RAW, JPEG, OR BOTH?

In the early days of digital photography, working with RAW image files and undertaking the often time-consuming process of developing them on a computer was the norm. A lot has changed since then. The exceptional and widely respected quality of JPEG images produced by Fujifilm X-Series cameras means photographers have access to superb photos right out of the camera. The X-Trans sensor is the main engine behind the excellent color reproduction, genuine film-like appearance, and digital grain (attractive noise) in images taken by X-Series cameras. You have three options when it comes to selecting a file type for saving your images: JPEG, RAW, or RAW+JPEG. The key consideration is whether you have the time, know-how, and desire to convert RAW files.

RAW conversion, which is equivalent to developing film in a chemical darkroom, lets you engage with your images in the digital darkroom to get the most out of them. You can change the exposure by several stops, modify the white balance, and alter a variety of color characteristics, including film simulation, contrast, tone curve, and several other parameters, before you save the file as a JPEG or a TIFF. There is no loss of image quality when you work with RAW files, whereas JPEG files suffer quality losses when they are edited. In addition to Silkypix, the RAW conversion software that comes with the camera, other popular programs—such as Photoshop, Lightroom, and Capture One—can convert Fujifilm RAW files, which have the file name extension RAF.

There is no reason not to capture images as JPEGs as long as the shooting settings were configured properly and the exposure is accurate. If you are working at an event and have customers who want images to take with them, JPEGs are the only way to go. In more critical situations that may require substantive editing and image optimization after the shoot, it makes more sense to save your images as RAW or RAW+JPEG.

Aside from the standard 3:2 and 4:3 aspect ratios, square (1:1) and panorama formats are also available. Because we live in an age of increasingly better and larger storage media, it makes sense to always shoot with Fine image quality; it offers the highest quality with the least compression. The 3:2 aspect ratio is the natural choice given the dimensions of the APS-C sensor (23.6mm x 15.6mm). The other available formats are created by internal cropping. Table 2.2 shows the image capacity for an 8 GB SD memory card based on different size and quality settings.

File Type	Medium JPEG	Large JPEG	RAW
Size	3456 × 2304 (3:2)	4896 × 3264 (3:2)	4896 × 3264 (3:2)
Quality	FINE	FINE	— (RAW)
SDHC card	1,600 images	800 images	230 images

Table 2.2: Card capacity, depending on image size

If you were to shoot with the smallest image size (S) and the highest image quality (Fine), an 8 GB SD card could hold 3,030 images. I recommend using several smaller-capacity memory cards to avoid having all your images on one physical device. The data security on modern storage devices is continuously improving, but it is always wise to have a sound and reliable backup strategy.

THE X-TRANS SENSOR

The construction of the X-Trans CMOS sensor is remarkable. Let's dive into the details about what makes it such a powerful sensor.

The Fujifilm X100T employs the new and improved X-Trans CMOS II sensor.

The sensor's excellent image quality results, in part, from two traits: first, it doesn't have a low-pass filter, which is traditionally used to minimize moiré effects in conventional systems at the expense of resolution; and second, it has a unique pixel arrangement.

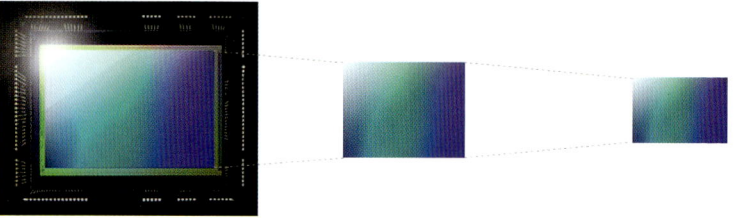

Figure 2.18: Sensor sizes, from left to right: APS-C (23.6mm x 15.6mm), Micro Four Thirds (17mm x 13mm), 1-inch (13.2mm x 8.8mm)

Most sensors are covered with an array of colored filters called a Bayer pattern (named after Bryce E. Bayer, who patented the technology on March 5, 1975, in the name of Eastman Kodak). The surface of the filter is divided into a regular pattern of three colors: 50% of the pattern is green, 25% is red, and 25% is blue. The design mimics the makeup of color film, which has a celluloid backing with layers of photosensitive silver halide crystals. These crystals are the analog equivalent of pixels on a digital sensor, but the crystals are distributed irregularly and do not have a repeating pattern. As a result, film is not susceptible to the moiré effect, which compromises the quality of images that include fine patterns of lines or dots. Because digital images are susceptible to the moiré effect, the inclusion of miniscule repeating patterns is an attempt to replicate the way film works and minimize the problem.

Figure 2.19: Film under an electron microscope

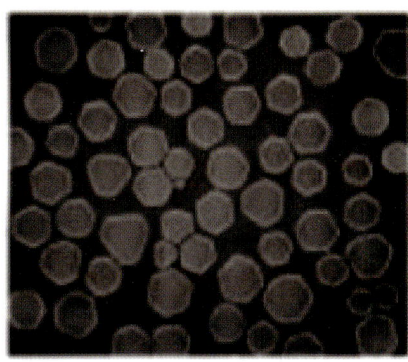

Mass producing a sensor with an organic, irregular pattern would be prohibitively expensive, but fortunately a 6 x 6 pattern, instead of the conventional 2 x 2 Bayer pattern, is an effective approximation of film. This pattern minimizes the moiré effect and maximizes sensor resolution.

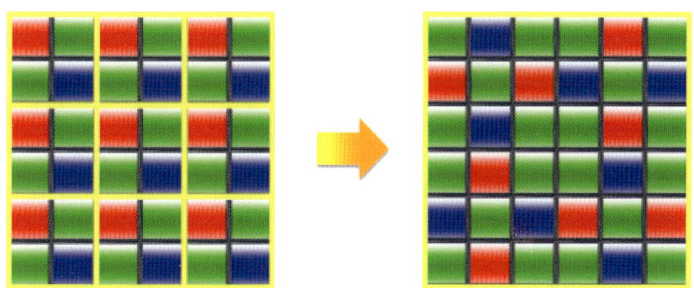

Figure 2.20: A Bayer pattern (left) compared to the X-Trans sensor's 6 x 6 pattern (right)

As with the Bayer pattern, green is the dominant color of the X-Trans filter. Human eyesight is particularly sensitive to green tones, which influence how people perceive brightness, contrast, and sharpness in both color and black-and-white photography. Distinguishing among tones of gray is directly related to our heightened sensitivity for green.

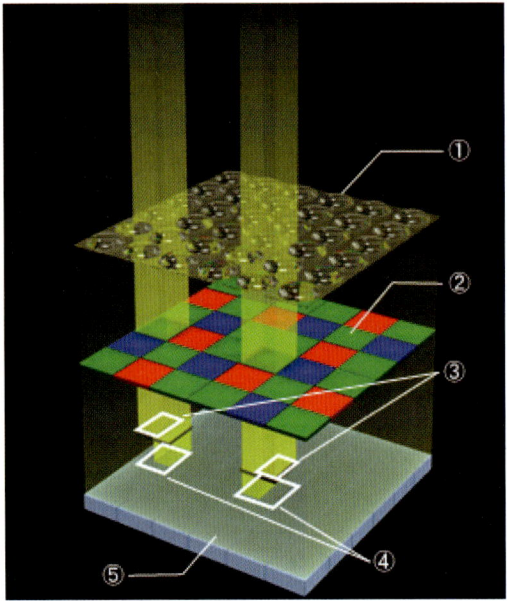

1 Microlenses
2 X-Trans color filter
3 L/R light interception filter
4 Phase-detection sensor
5 Photodiode

Figure 2.21:
The anatomy of an
X-Trans II sensor

Phase-detection pixels are integrated directly into the pixel array to improve the speed of the autofocus system. The EXR Processor II and the lens modulation optimizer (LMO) technology dramatically improve lens aberrations (e.g., diffraction blur) and produce images that have improved sharpness and more natural color reproduction.

2.5 White Balance

To adjust a camera's white balance, you calibrate the sensor to the color temperature of the ambient light. If you know the actual color temperature for a specific light source, you can manually enter the value (in kelvin, the unit of measure for color temperature that describes the color of light) in the camera. The automatic white balance system usually produces good results, but there are two caveats: (1) if there are large bright areas in the scene, the camera will assume they are white or neutral gray; and (2) auto white balance often assumes that an image should contain an equal distribution of colors, which can lead to an unwanted color cast in subjects that don't feature all colors or that are predominantly one color. Human vision makes a similar adjustment, called chromatic adaptation.

In addition to entering a color temperature value, you can choose one of the following options from the camera's white balance menu: auto white balance, sun/daylight, shade, daylight fluorescent, warm white florescent, cool white florescent, incandescent, underwater, and manual white balance.

Manual white balance is the best bet if you're trying to reproduce natural color in your image. To set the white balance, select the manual option from the white balance menu, frame a white balance card so it fills most of the image area, and take a picture under the ambient lighting conditions. The camera stores this shot as a reference and uses it for subsequent exposures.

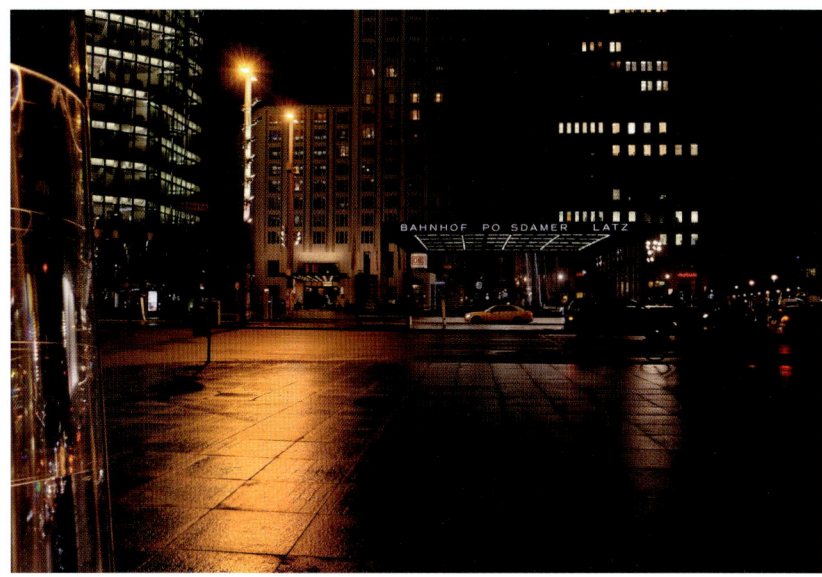

Figure 2.22: **Custom white balance at 6700 K**

In most situations you'll probably want to capture natural-looking colors, but sometimes you may want to skew the white balance to produce a special effect, such as a warm or cool appearance. Navigate to menu Red 3.1 to manually enter a white balance value. You can program the color temperature in 100-degree increments from 2000 K to 15,000 K. If you want to inspect the results of the white balance setting in real time, make sure that Preview Pic. Effect is turned on (Blue 2.3.9). Depending on the subject and your intentions, you can create stylized images without post-processing.

2.6 Film Simulations and Advanced Filters

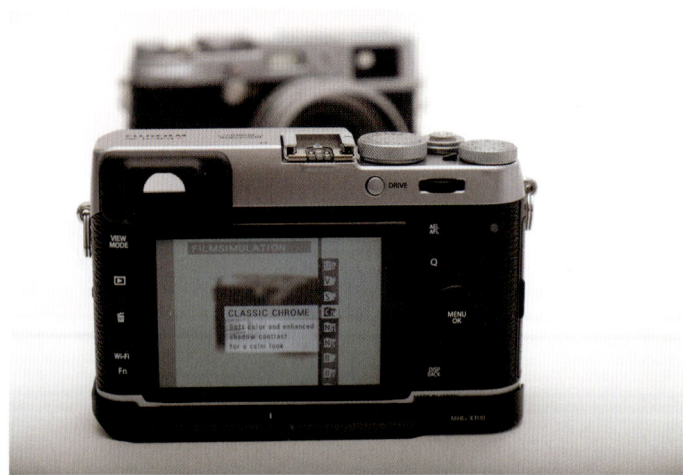

Figure 2.23: **The Film Simulation menu**

In film photography, the first thing photographers have to consider is what type of film to use. Each type of film has specific characteristics for color reproduction, contrast, sensitivity, and grain. In digital photography, many serious amateur and professional photographers modulate these variables by shooting in RAW format and using settings that retain as much visual data as possible so they have maximum flexibility during post-processing to create the look they want. Although this requires a good deal of time and know-how, it allows photographers to produce excellent results that are generally superior to standard JPEGs that are generated by the camera.

Here's where the Fujifilm film simulations come into play. Many archives feature stores of Velvia or Provia slides, to name just two of the many types of film that were once widely popular. Fujifilm has succeeded in transferring the visual feel of these film types—and many others—into the digital world with film simulations. These simulations don't just make an image appear slightly more colorful or less colorful by adjusting saturation levels. Table 2.3 lists the key characteristics of the various film simulations that are available in the X100T and X100S. And figure 2.24 shows various film simulations applied to the same landscape photograph.

Camera Model	Film Simulation	Characteristics
X100T	Classic Chrome	Based loosely on the color reproduction of Kodachrome 64
X100S and X100T	Provia	Standard contrasts with moderate saturation
X100S and X100T	Velvia	Very contrasty with high color saturation
X100S and X100T	Astia	Between Provia and Velvia in terms of contrast, attractive skin tones
X100S and X100T	Pro Neg. Std	Lowest contrast and most neutral, making it the preferred choice for many RAW shooters
X100S and X100T	Pro Neg. Hi	Slightly more pronounced contrast compared to Astia
X100S and X100T	Monochrome	Black-and-white
X100S and X100T	Monochrome plus yellow filter	Subtle contrast boost
X100S and X100T	Monochrome plus green filter	Softened skin tones and improved reproduction of green tones
X100S and X100T	Monochrome plus red filter	Darkened exposure of sky
X100S and X100T	Sepia	Sepia-tinged images

Table 2.3: Film simulations of the X100T and X100S

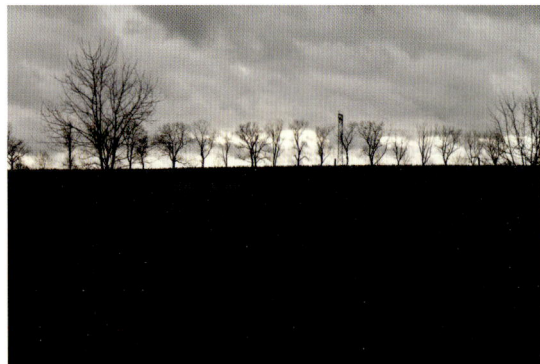

Classic Chrome

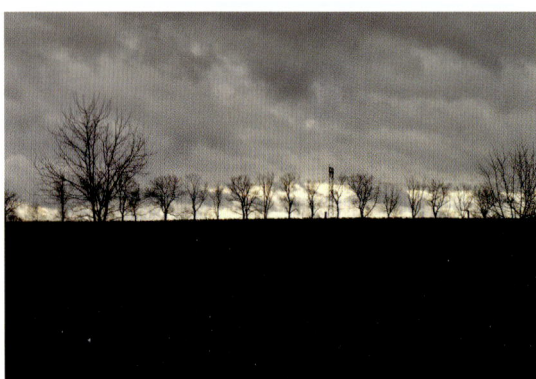

Provia

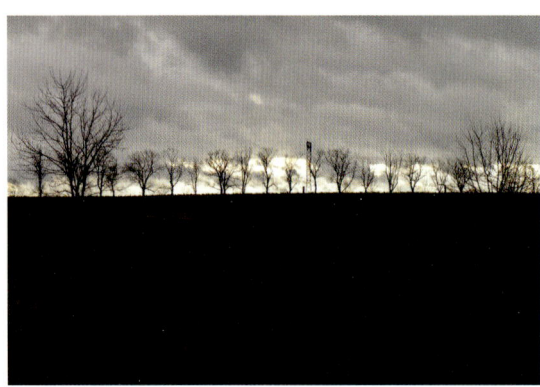

Velvia

Astia

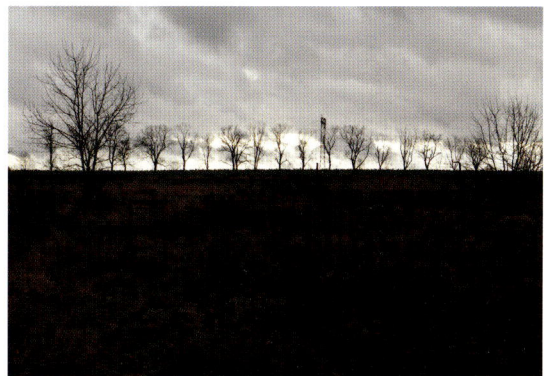

Pro Neg. Hi

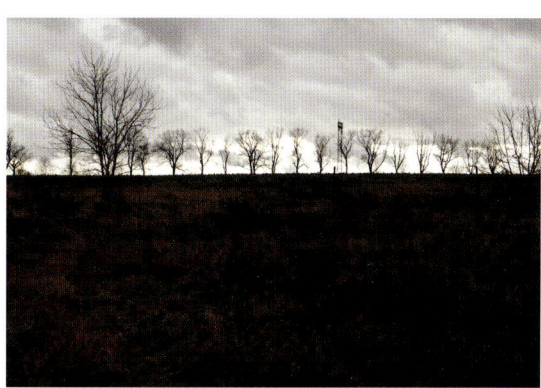

Pro Neg. Standard

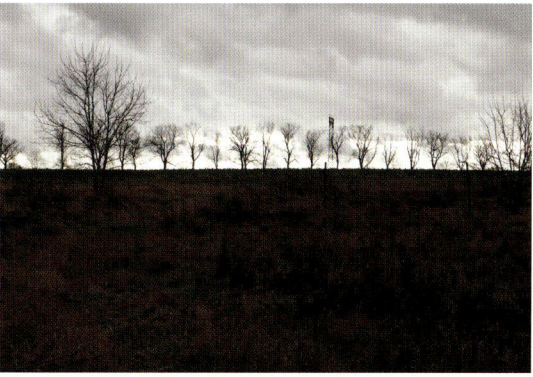

Figure 2.24: Comparison of film simulations with white balance set to shade

When you shoot with black-and-white film simulations, you can apply yellow, green, and red filters to affect the appearance of gray tones. Colors that match the filter color are intensified or brightened, and complementary colors are suppressed or darkened.

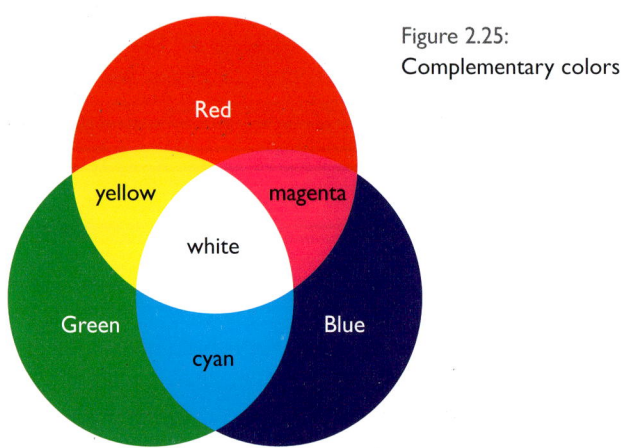

Figure 2.25:
Complementary colors

The yellow filter boosts contrast somewhat and will slightly darken the brightness of the sky and reduce atmospheric haze. The yellow and green filters are favorites for portraiture because they tend to soften skin tones and minimize skin imperfections. In landscape and nature photography, the green filter accentuates subtle green tones in foliage by simultaneously darkening red tones. The red filter has a relatively pronounced effect, especially in landscape photography on sunny days, because it darkens the blue sky and makes it possible to capture an image with a dramatic range of contrast.

Monochrome

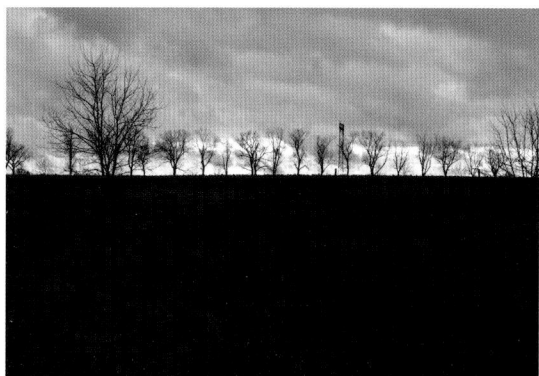

Monochrome with
yellow filter

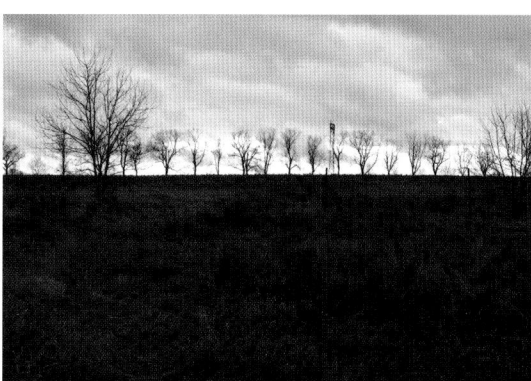

Monochrome with
red filter

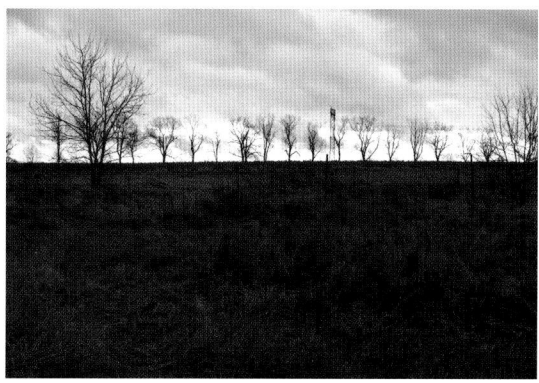

Figure 2.26: Monochrome film simulations
(continues on next page)

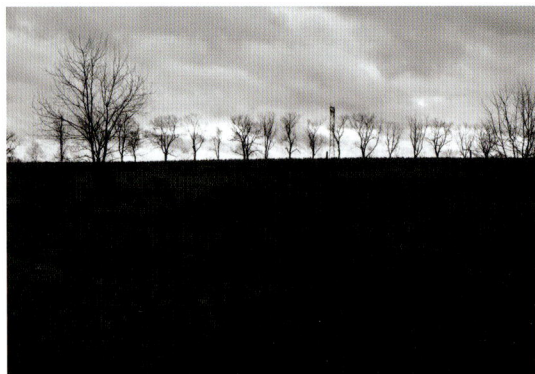

Monochrome with
green filter

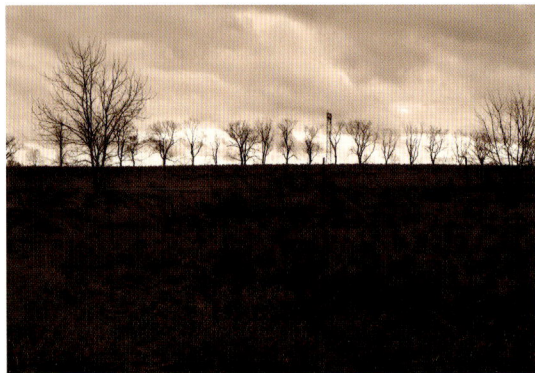

Sepia

ADVANCED FILTERS

The Fujifilm X100T comes with 13 creative filters. You can see the effects of the filters on your images when they are displayed on the camera's LCD monitor. The menu at Red 4.1 gives you the options described in Table 2.4.

Toy Camera	Shaded, slightly darker image borders that mimic toy cameras or pinhole cameras
Miniature	Blurring in the top and bottom of the image area to produce a miniature, or diorama, effect
Pop Color	Very contrasty with saturated colors

High-Key	Increased brightness and reduced contrast; particularly suited for bright tonal values
Low-Key	Uniform dark tones with minimal highlights
Dynamic Tone	Tone expression to create a fantasy look
Soft Focus	Uniform softening across the image area
Partial Color (Red)	Red tones retain color; all other tones are rendered in black-and-white
Partial Color (Orange)	Orange tones retain color; all other tones are rendered in black-and-white
Partial Color (Yellow)	Yellow tones retain color; all other tones are rendered in black-and-white
Partial Color (Green)	Green tones retain color; all other tones are rendered in black-and-white
Partial Color (Blue)	Blue tones retain color; all other tones are rendered in black-and-white
Partial Color (Purple)	Purple tones retain color; all other tones are rendered in black-and-white

Table 2.4: Advanced filters for creative effects

These special effects allow you to produce stylized images directly from your camera, which you may find useful if you want to print pictures on the fly, such as with a Fujifilm Instax printer. The usefulness of these effects filters varies depending on individual needs. For example, the black-and-white filters with partial coloration don't appeal to me much, but I enjoy using the Toy Camera, High-Key, and Low-Key filters from time to time for snapshots. It's worth experimenting with them a little to see if you like them.

2.7 Dynamic Range, Highlights and Shadows, and Sharpness

The most basic way to define dynamic range is to describe it as the difference in brightness from the darkest to brightest parts of an image. As it relates to a digital camera, in technical terms dynamic range describes the maximum range of brightness values that can be reproduced without losing detail in the darkest or brightest parts of the scene. In digital photography, there are two common problems: very dark areas of the captured scene are dominated by the noise of the sensor, and very bright areas appear as pure white patches that contain no structure or details. Any time the dynamic range of the camera is smaller, or narrower, than that of the scene, information is lost. We all know from experience that an overcast day poses few, if any, problems when taking pictures, while shooting on a bright and sunny day in an environment with lots of shadow and direct sunlight often makes us squint our eyes, let alone allow for a properly exposed image. The range of brightness values from dark to light is just too large.

In order to quantify dynamic range, the actual brightness values of the dark and light parts of an image are described in terms of a ratio, and then that ratio can be described in terms of f-stops, or light values. For example, let's say "1" is assigned to the darkest part of an image, while "2" is assigned to that part of the image that's twice as bright. For these two values, this gives us a contrast ratio of 2:1. A contrast ratio of 1,024:1 is, therefore, equivalent to a dynamic range of 10 f-stops because 2^{10} = 1,024. In order to put this in perspective, one should know that the human eye can cover a range of up to 14 f-stops, a classic black and white analog film covers up to 11 f-stops, a modern digital camera covers up to 10 f-stops, analog color film covers around 8 f-stops, and

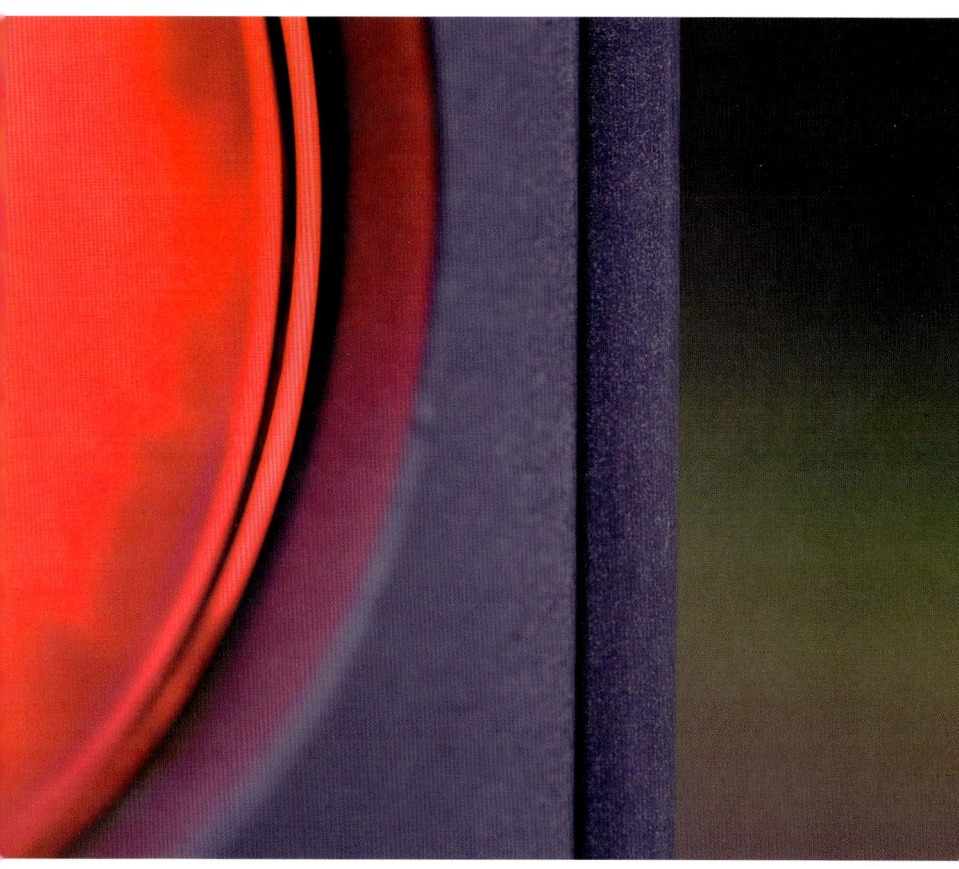

a printed photograph on glossy paper covers around 7 f-stops. At the end of the day, recording the image is one thing. The bottleneck comes when we look at an image on paper or on our computer screens. An active matrix display covers around 8 f-stops while many "standard displays" perform quite a bit worse. These days, everybody talks about 4k and 8k technology. Apart from ultra-high resolution, extending the dynamic range of these new displays will be exceedingly important.

The ISO 100 setting on the X100T and X100S allows photographers to shoot with a low level of image noise, but it sacrifices dynamic range. Pictures shot at this ISO sensitivity will be effectively overexposed by one stop, with some clipping of the highlights at the same time.

DYNAMIC RANGE SETTINGS

Now that we've discussed dynamic range theory, it's time to think about which contrast settings to use in specific shooting situations. The Fujifilm X100T has the same four dynamic range (DR) settings as those of its predecessors: DR 100%, which is the baseline default; DR 200%, which extends the dynamic range by one stop; DR 400%, which extends the dynamic range by two stops; and Auto DR, which automatically determines the dynamic range within certain limits. The extended dynamic range options allow you to capture more detail in the highlights or the bright areas of the image. Choosing DR 200% causes the camera to darken the exposure by one stop; choosing DR 400% darkens the exposure by two stops. The minimum ISO values for shooting with these contrast-extension settings are 400 and 800, respectively. The camera's internal image-developing process uses sophisticated tone mapping to adjust the middle and dark tones back to their normal brightness. The signal amplification is reduced by one (DR 200%) or two (DR 400%) exposure values. Photographers who shoot exclusively in JPEG format benefit from the fact that the camera always applies the 4,096 tonal values of RAW data (12 bit) and reduces the output image to 8-bit format only when it saves the image. RAW shooters will end up with a picture that is one or two stops (DR 200% or DR 400%, respectively) underexposed and is subsequently processed with the camera's internal methods. When you open the file with the Silkypix RAW converter, the software will recognize the DR function and make corresponding suggestions for improvements. You can then apply your own tone mapping edits and make additional adjustments.

I often shoot in RAW+JPEG mode so I can have both high-quality JPEG files with my preferred film simulation applied and digital negatives that I can develop and edit as I choose. To achieve the optimal exposure for my intended purposes, I choose the DR mode on a case-by-case basis.

DR 200% is an ideal option for subjects that have a relatively broad contrast range because it is a decent compromise between maximizing detail in the darkest and lightest areas of the image and retaining a high level of image quality. Subjects with more dramatic contrast ranges may require DR 400%. I like to refer to this function as "HDR light" because it produces great results when full HDR isn't necessary or practical. Should you always enable the extended dynamic range features? The answer is a resounding no. Many subjects fall within the contrast limits that the sensor can capture. When a subject's contrast range is smaller than the camera's dynamic range, the dynamic range extension options negatively influence image quality because the camera will underexpose photos by one (DR 200%) or two (DR 400%) stops. As previously mentioned, the lower register of the dynamic range is less capable of reproducing details and the full tonal range, and the signal-to-noise ratio is greater.

For the most part, Auto DR is good at discerning when and how to employ the extended dynamic range options. There are, however, a few situations that raise red flags. Consider, for example, a monotone gray sky that is uniformly bright and lacks even a single cloud with an interesting shape or texture that is worth capturing. The extended dynamic range options won't rescue any details in the highlights, but they will negatively affect the shadows. You would be better off shooting with DR 100% and using a standard exposure compensation adjustment with a careful eye toward detail reproduction in the shadows.

For those of you who make use of the histogram in the viewfinder or on the LCD, there is an important difference between the X100T and X100S when it comes to the DR function. Let's have a look at the X100T first: With the Display Custom Settings "Histogram" and "Dynamic Range" (Menu Red 3.5) activated, we get the correct live histogram and information about which DR setting is used. Having a dominant peak on the very right side of the histogram would indicate a severely overexposed highlight section of the image. Trying to go to DR 200% or DR 400% instead of DR 100% could potentially solve the problem or suggest a different exposure setting. Turning the exposure compensation dial, for example, will give you immediate feedback.

On the X100S: With the Display Custom Settings "Histogram" and "Dynamic Range" (Menu Red 3.4) activated, the live histogram that is shown does not imply the actual DR setting; it always shows the histogram for the basic DR 100% setting. One way to pre-check the image with the help of the histogram before actually taking the photograph would be to point the camera toward the brightest areas of the frame in order to determine the targeted exposure and then apply any necessary adjustments.

DR=100%
The highlights are clipped as shown on the right side of the histogram. The shadows have detail.

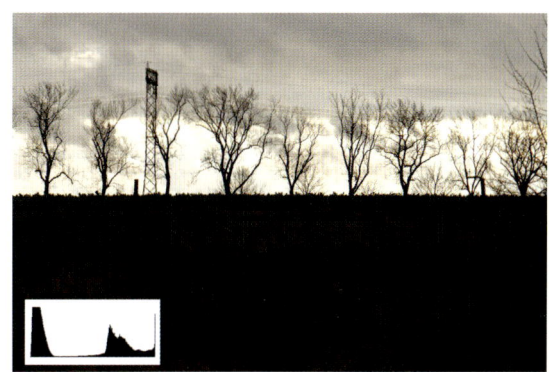

DR=200%
Almost all the highlights are rescued, and the detail in the shadows is comparable to the picture above.

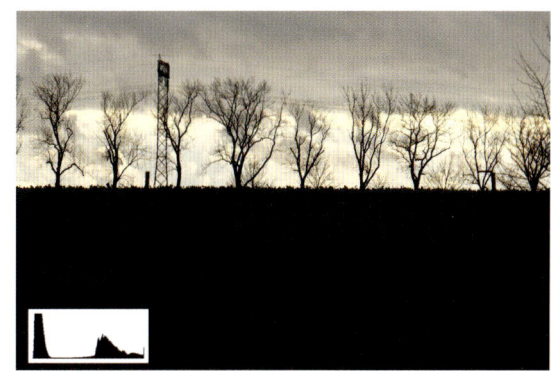

DR=400%
All the details in the highlights are visible. The shadows (the meadow in the foreground) still have a sufficient level of detail.

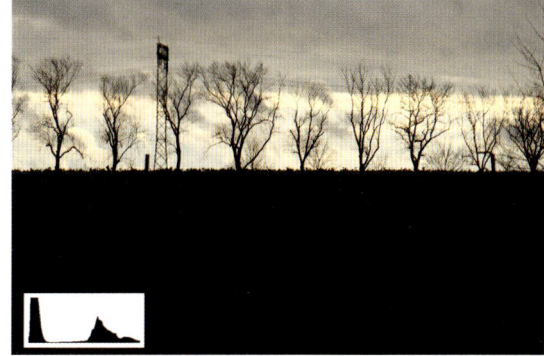

Figure 2.27: Comparing DR 100%, DR 200%, and DR 400%

I advise against adjusting the sharpness or contrast with the Q menu because it's difficult to assess the impact of the adjustments while you're shooting. An adjustment of +1 or −2 may look fine on the camera LCD monitor, but you could be in for an unpleasant surprise when you take a closer look on your computer monitor. When it comes to Highlight Tone and Shadow Tone, which you access at menus Red 2.4 and Red 2.5, it's a different story. These controls allow you to make subtle adjustments to the highlights and shadows in an image. These adjustments are comparable to bending the curve when you map tones in Photoshop. That is, a slight S-shaped curve increases the contrast without affecting the black and white points in the image. For example, with a Shadow Tone setting of +1 and a Highlight Tone setting of −1, the darkest areas (RGB 0,0,0) and the brightest areas (RGB 255,255,255) of the image remain unchanged, but the detail contrast in the shadows is increased and the highlights are softened. You might save a shooting profile (Edit/Save Custom Setting at menu Red 3.3) with Monochrome set to Red Filter, Shadow Tone set to +1, and Highlight Tone set to +1 for taking high-contrast black-and-white images. Alternatively, you could add these two functions to the Q menu for easy access. Figure 2.28 shows the effect of adjusting these settings.

Shadow: Standard (0)
Highlight: Standard (0)

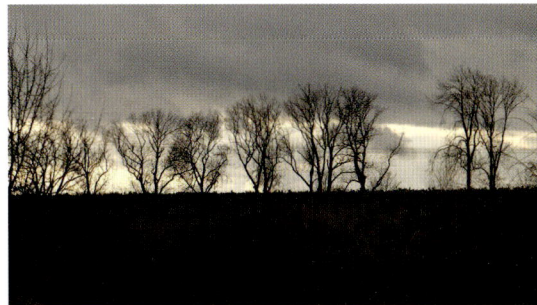

Shadow:
Medium Soft (−1)
Highlight:
Medium Hard (+1)

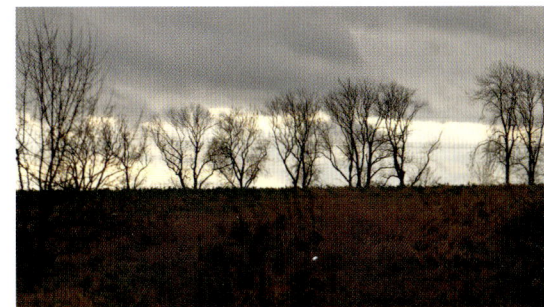

Shadow: Soft (−2)
Highlight: Hard (+2)

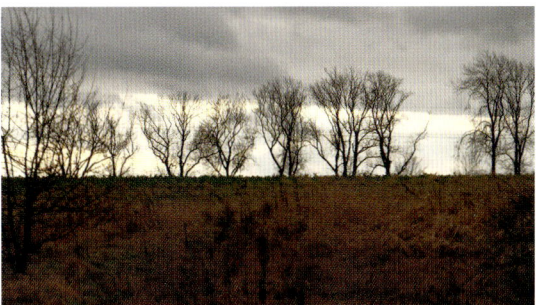

Figure 2.28: Adjustments to shadows and highlights

The first picture, which is the result of the standard settings for highlight and shadow tone, has a very dark foreground. Increasing the Highlight Tone setting by increasing degrees brightens the image dramatically and reveals more detail. Of the three images in this series, the middle one is my favorite.

2.8 In-Camera Image Editing

The X100T and X100S come equipped with a powerful RAW conversion feature that can adjust the exposure by −1 to +1 EV in increments of 1/3 EV (similar to push and pull in film developing), change the white balance, fine-tune the highlights and shadows, and evaluate film simulations while you look at an image on the camera's LCD monitor. These functions are particularly valuable in that they allow you to get a rough impression of the RAW exposure while shooting or immediately afterward, or so that you can send a printable version of the image to a portable printer, such as a Fujifilm Instax.

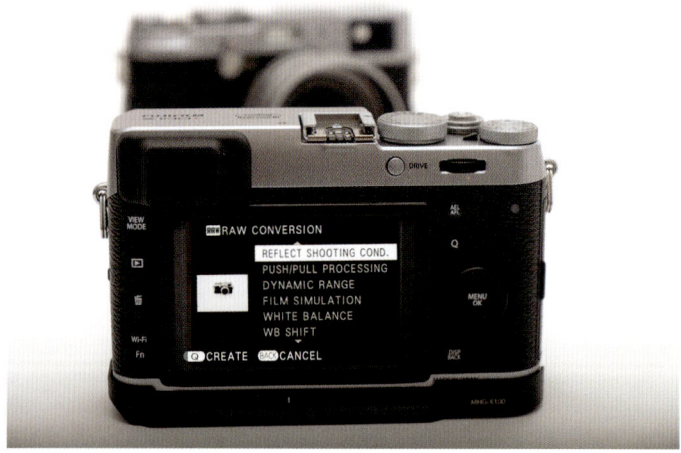

Figure 2.29: Internal RAW file conversion

2.9 Wi-Fi Functionality

X100T

Unlike the X100S, the X100T offers Wi-Fi functionality.

The Camera Remote app from Fujifilm (for iOS and Android) allows you to transfer images directly from the camera to a smartphone or tablet, where they can be edited, published to the web, or printed. Perhaps of greater interest is the wide array of options that the app offers for remotely adjusting camera settings, including focus, shutter release for stills and video, aperture, shutter speed, exposure compensation, ISO sensitivity, film simulation, white balance, macro functionality, self-timer, and flash control. It may be helpful to transfer image files directly to your computer in some situations, but the slow data transfer speed somewhat limits this feature. The menu function at Blue 3.2.2 allows you to transfer larger files when you shoot in RAW+JPEG mode.

Wi-Fi transmitter	Standard IEEE 802.11b/g/n (standard wireless protocol) Access mode Infrastructure
Wi-Fi functionality	Geotagging, wireless communication (image transfer), viewing images, remote camera operation, connect to Instax printers, PC auto save

Table 2.5: Wi-Fi functionality

The various wireless functions described here sound easy enough to use, but establishing a connection between your camera and your smartphone or tablet can sometimes be challenging. Follow these steps closely: First, activate the Wi-Fi functionality on your camera, then on your smartphone or tablet. After a few seconds, a wireless network called Fujifilm should appear. Select that network. After a connection is established, you can start the Fujifilm app, and everything should be up and running. If the connection doesn't seem to be working, go through the steps again.

REMOTE CONTROL

Android users should be sure to install version 4.0 or higher for the remote control function to work. Also note that Fujifilm offers more than one app; install Camera Remote, not Camera Application. Android users may also want to use a Wi-Fi manager so it's easy to identify your camera among other networks and devices that may appear. It's a bit easier for iPhone users; select X100T under Settings > Wi-Fi to establish the wireless connection. You can name your camera by navigating to Wireless Settings > General Settings > Name. Make sure to set your camera to the desired exposure mode first because it can't be controlled with the app. A good option for most situations is to use manual exposure mode with a defined aperture and shutter speed. The fully automatic exposure mode is shown as P in the app; in this mode, your control of the exposure is limited to exposure compensation.

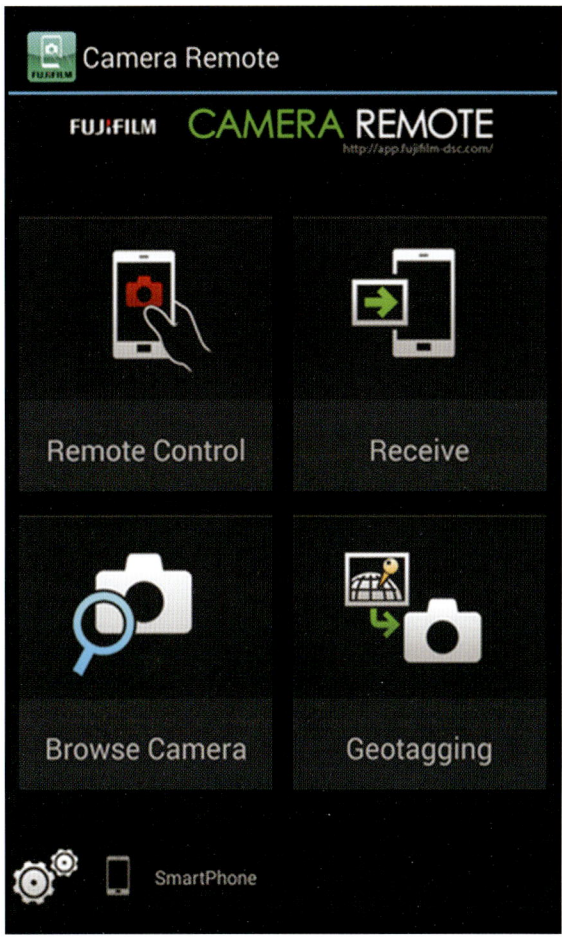

You must turn on your camera's Wi-Fi functionality before you can connect it to your smartphone or tablet. After it is on, the Wi-Fi icon will blink while a connection is established. Deactivate all other networks on your smartphone or tablet, then select the X100T. Next, launch the Fujifilm Camera Remote app. After the connection is established, the camera display will turn off, and the screen on your remote device will display a live view of the subject. At this point you can control the exposure settings exclusively with the remote device; with the exception of the On/Off switch, all the camera controls will be disabled. If the wireless connection is lost and your camera freezes, you have to turn your camera off and restart it.

FILE TRANSFER

The Camera Remote app can wirelessly transfer images to your remote device without a password. You can seamlessly shoot, transfer, and upload your new masterpieces to Facebook or Twitter for the world to see. The time required to transfer an image depends on the file size, but you can use the Resize Image for Smartphone option on the Wireless Settings menu (Blue 3.2) to expedite the process. Use the previously described steps to establish a wireless connection, then scroll through your pictures and press OK when you find one you want to transfer. After you transfer an image, you can continue scrolling and transferring by pressing the Selector button again. You can terminate the connection by pressing the Display/Back button.

BROWSING THE CAMERA WITH A SMARTPHONE

This feature allows you to scroll through the pictures on your camera with your remote device and select multiple files to transfer at one time. Images with a question mark will not be transferred. Note that video should be recorded in HD (1280 x 720) or smaller, and the ability to view video on the remote device depends on the functionality of the apps that are installed.

GEOTAGGING

When you sync your smartphone with your camera, you can use your phone's GPS functionality to automatically write location coordinates into the EXIF file of your RAW or JPEG images; this process is known as geotagging. To enable this function, navigate to menu Blue 3.4, where you

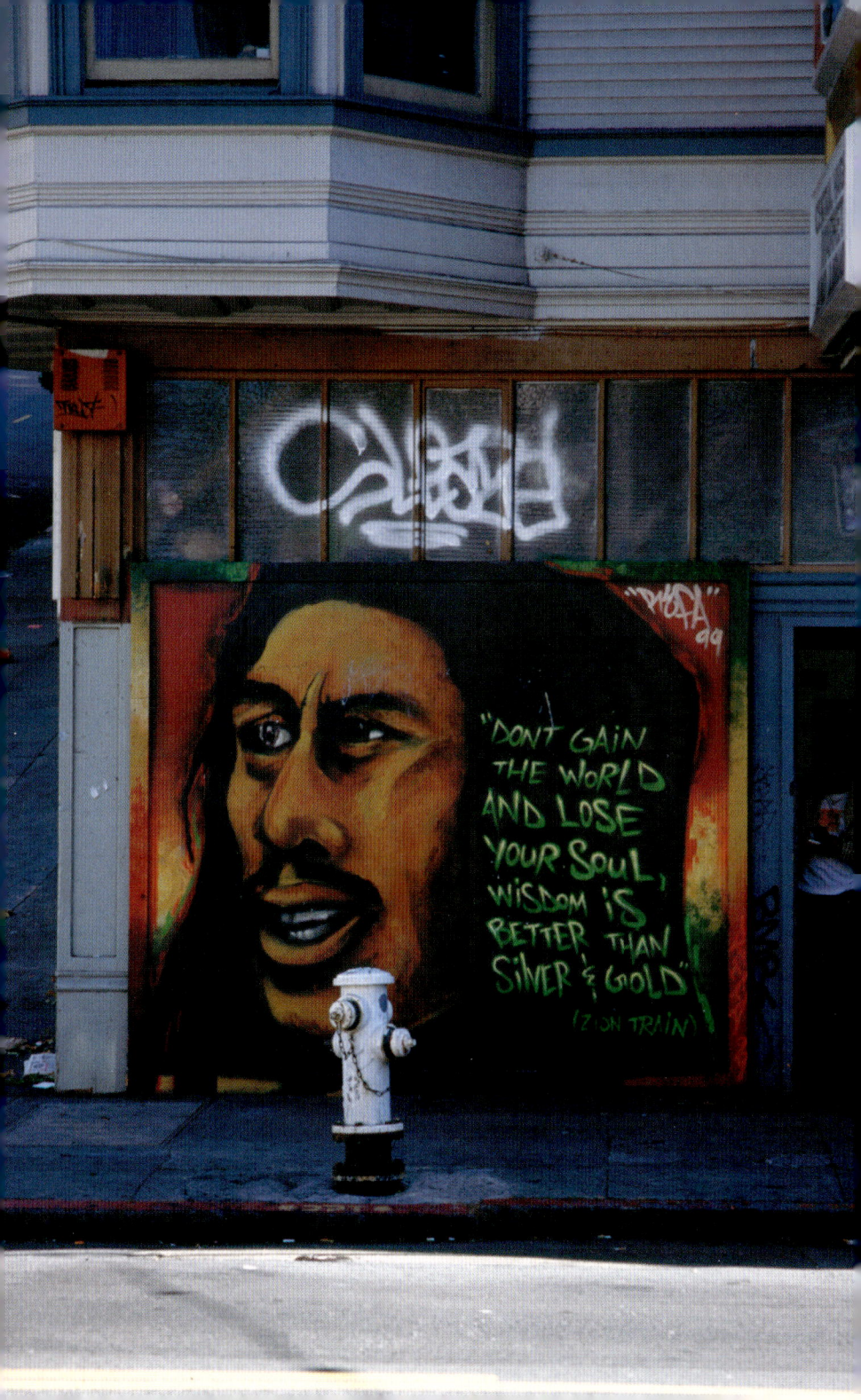

will find Geotagging Set-Up. If you want to view the co-ordinate data on your camera, you can turn Location Info on. After the location data is successfully transferred from your phone to your camera, you can end the wireless connection because the coordinate information will be saved for three hours. If you want to update the location information—perhaps you're on a road trip and your location is constantly changing—simply reestablish the connection. After the location information has been transferred, your device will display a message saying that the location data upload is complete, and you're back in business. If you're using an iPhone, the connection automatically ends after the information is successfully transferred.

2.10 Flash Photography

The built-in Super Intelligent Flash feature produces a highly serviceable fill flash, but it isn't ideal if you need indirect flash or a brighter output. Fujifilm offers three external flash units (EF-20, EF-X20, and EF-42), and thanks to the leaf shutter in the X100T and X100s, sync speeds up to 1/4000 second are possible. The "sync speed" is the shortest possible shutter speed that allows the shutter to be completely open while the flash fully illuminates the sensor. The flash fires when the shutter is fully open, and this camera's fastest sync speed (1/4000 second) is nearly 10 times faster than that of many DSLRs. Focal-plane shutters in DSLRs are susceptible to flash complications that leaf shutters avoid. When you take a picture with a shutter speed that is technically faster than the time the shutter can actually be fully open all at once, the second curtain of a focal-plane shutter starts to follow the first curtain across the sensor, creating a traveling slit that permits light to reach the sensor (the faster the shutter speed, the narrower the slit). If the flash fires during this process, shadows will appear in the exposure where the second curtain covers the sensor.

As with the other cameras in the Fujifilm X-Series, you can use third-party flash units as long as you're willing to forego electronic through-the-lens (TTL) metering. At first it may seem undesirable to use a third-party flash unit, but unlike many other photographers, I think manual flash control is the best option. The main problem with relying on semiautomatic flash control is that slight changes in the lighting or minor adjustments to the shooting location can result in entirely different metering results, which can cause the camera to expose images with varying degrees of influence from the flash. As an example, imagine that you're photographing a baptism in a church. There are no windows near the subject, and the environment is quite dark. To capture all the action, including quick movements without blur, you have to select a sufficiently fast shutter speed, such as 1/125 second. You may need to select an aperture between f/2.8 and f/4 to get the depth of field you want. At ISO 3200 the image is slightly underexposed, but it's adequately sharp and the colors are saturated. Increasing the ISO to 6400 would produce a brighter image, but the background elements would be too bright. Here's where it makes sense to use an external flash, manually reduce its power to 1/4 or 1/8 of its maximum output, and keep that setting fixed. You can bounce the flash off the ceiling or soften its light another way to achieve flattering illumination for people's faces and create a pleasant glow in their eyes while avoiding shadows. This approach would also allow the church windows in the background to appear attractively in the image. You can take one or two test shots to find the correct flash output, then you only have to wait for the right moment to capture the picture. The overall lighting situation won't change, so you don't have to make further adjustments to the flash exposure settings. All your pictures will exhibit the same brightness, so you can choose the sharpest image with the best composition from the shoot. It won't be necessary to post-process your images to correct exposure errors.

X100T

You cannot use the built-in flash or an external flash unit with the electronic shutter.

Navigate to menu Red 5.3 (Flash Mode) to select one of the flash options: Forced Flash, Commander, External Flash, and Suppressed Flash. As the name implies, Forced Flash causes the flash to fire for every exposure, which is practical when you are shooting backlit subjects and want a balanced exposure in the foreground. This flash mode requires the shutter speed to be 1/30 second or faster.

The Commander flash mode allows you to use the built-in flash as a master to remotely trigger an external flash, such as the Fujifilm EF-X20 or any third-party flash that is equipped with remote functionality. Although Commander mode can cause the auxiliary flash to fire, it cannot control the flash output because there is no mechanism to detect ambient light and flash light; the camera sensor performs this function.

If you're shooting in Program AE (P) mode, where the camera automatically selects the aperture and shutter speed (which have both been set to A), you have two options in the Flash Mode menu: Auto and Slow Synchro. Predictably, in Auto mode, the camera determines when and how to fire the flash for each capture. Slow Synchro allows you to use shutter speeds slower than 1/30 second, a feature that may be useful for getting a balanced exposure for both a main subject in the foreground and background elements when you are shooting in low-light conditions.

Use the External Flash mode when you use third-party flash units, such as Nikon or Canon units. In general, I recommend using units whose flash output can be manually controlled because it usually takes just one or two quick test shots to figure out the right flash settings.

The Nissin i40 flash unit hit the market in November 2014 and offers many attractive options. It features somewhat retro styling, can be pointed sideways or upwards, does not have displays or buttons, and can be fully controlled with two simple dials. The Menu dial allows you to choose Slave Film (SF) and Optic Slave modes, which cause the unit to operate like a traditional studio slave flash (set the master flash manually when you use this mode). Slave Digital (SD) corresponds to Optic Slave mode, so TTL preflashes are ignored (in this mode, you'll want the master flash to operate with TTL metering). Manual (M) mode allows you to set the flash output between full power (1/1) and 1/256 of full power (a range that is equivalent to eight stops). In Automatic (A) mode, the Fujifilm Super Intelligent Flash system regulates the flash entirely on its own. In TTL mode, the automatic functionality is used and has additional options so you can adjust the flash output from −2.0 to +2.0. If you use multiple flash units, you can control the various groups directly from your camera. The flash brightness can be dialed up or down by two stops at the Flash Compensation menu (Red 5.4). When you need a modest fill flash, you can reduce the flash output a little. Suppressed Flash mode prevents the flash from firing, regardless of the lighting conditions.

Another alternative is the Yongnuo YN560-III shoe-mount flash. Like the Yongnuo YN560-TX, the unit can be operated wirelessly. It features a guide number of 58 and can be precisely set between full power and 1/128 of the maximum brightness. You can also use a power pack to extend the battery life.

If you travel a lot or shoot outdoors, where you don't have access to a power outlet, you may be interested in Godox flash units, which don't require a suitcase full of spare batteries. The V860N has all the common flash unit features and a lithium ion battery that can fire about 650 times at full power.

It's likely that Fujifilm will soon release a high-end flash unit with a higher guide number and wireless functionality to compete with some of these more sophisticated units.

2.11 The Three Classic Focal Lengths

A common argument against purchasing a Fujifilm X100 series camera is the lack of flexibility when it comes to lens focal lengths. All the models feature a fast f/2, 23mm fixed focal length lens, which, because of the APS-C sensor, equates to a 35mm field of view on a full-frame camera. To achieve superb imaging performance with such a compact camera body, Fujifilm moved the rear lens group into the camera body. The sensor is tuned to pair with the lens, which allows for excellent image quality across the entire frame.

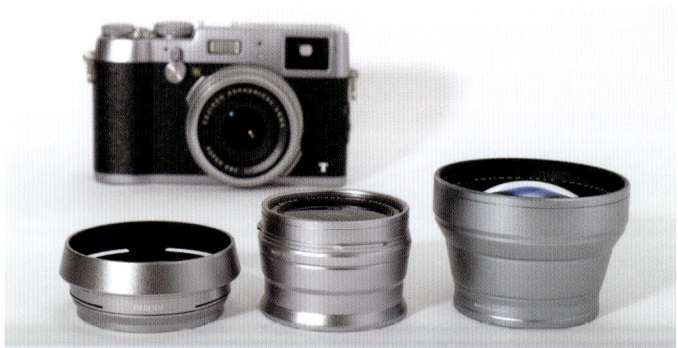

Figure 2.31: The lens hood, wide-angle lens, and teleconverter lens for the X100 cameras

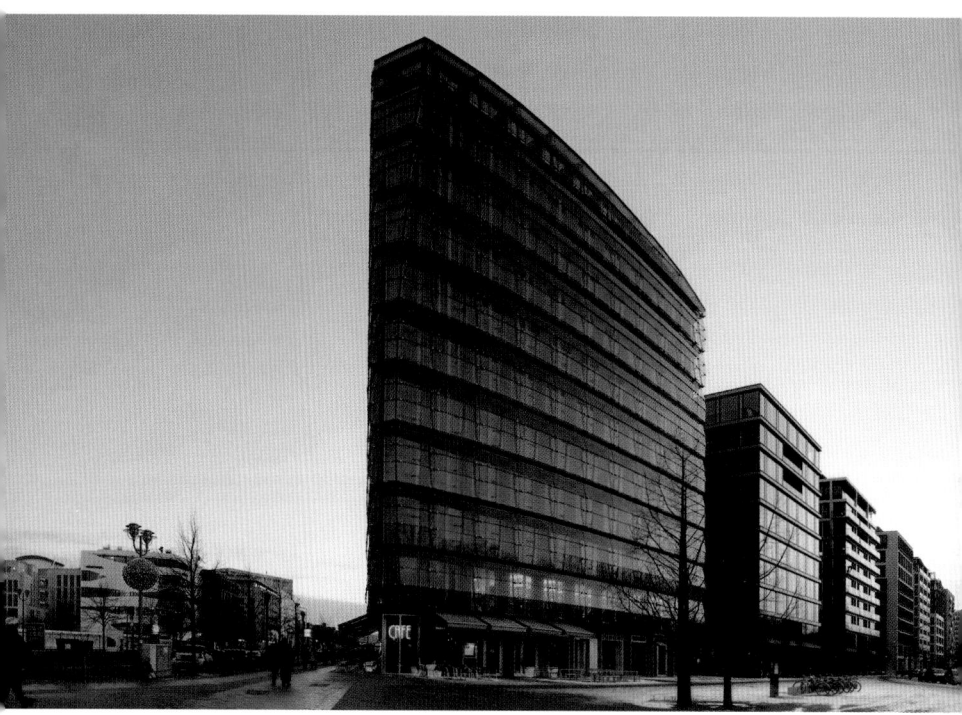

The built-in lens features eight elements in six groups arranged around a double-sided aspheric lens. All of the elements feature a high transmittance electron beam coating. The lens design offers truly amazing imaging performance with reduced ghosting and lens flare, minimal aberrations, top-notch sharpness, and balanced color reproduction. The mechanical aperture comprises nine blades; at its maximum opening it offers attractive background blur with crystal-clear sharpness in the focal area. The built-in focal length, traditionally associated with street photography and portraiture, can be modified with two conversion lenses so that effective focal lengths of 28mm, 35mm, and 50mm are at your disposal. Photographers who want to shoot at longer focal lengths are left to reach for a different camera. Because of their compact and elegant construction, the Fujifilm X100T and

X100S function as somewhat luxurious alternatives to the Fujinon XF 23mm lens for the Fujifilm X-Series cameras. The camera's internal ND filter permits photographers to reduce the intensity of the incident light by three stops (equivalent to 1/8 of the original incident light). This feature means you can shoot with a wide aperture in bright lighting or with backlit subjects and that you can photograph running water with a slow-enough shutter speed so it appears to have a smooth surface. The minimum focal distance is 10mm for closeup or macro shooting.

Wide-Angle Product Name	WCL-X100 S/B (Silver or Black)
Magnification	Approximately 0.8x
Effective focal length when affixed to an X100 camera	19mm (effectively 28mm with respect to 35mm format)
Configuration	4 elements in 3 groups
Mass	Approximately 150 g
Dimensions	55mm x 37mm
Filter diameter	49 mm

Teleconverter Product Name	TCL-X100 S/B (Silver or Black)
Magnification	Approximately 1.4x
Effective focal length when affixed to an X100 camera	33mm (effectively 50mm with respect to 35mm format)
Configuration	4 elements in 4 groups
Mass	Approximately 180 g
Dimensions	70mm x 46.5mm
Filter diameter	67mm

Table 2.6: Wide-angle (WCL-X100) and teleconverter (TCL-X100) lens specifications

Figure 2.32: Lens comparison with the Fujifilm X100T featuring the 28mm wide-angle lens, a standard 35mm field of view, and the 50mm teleconverter lens. Each image was shot from the same location. Camera settings were ISO 2500, f/4, 1/80 second.

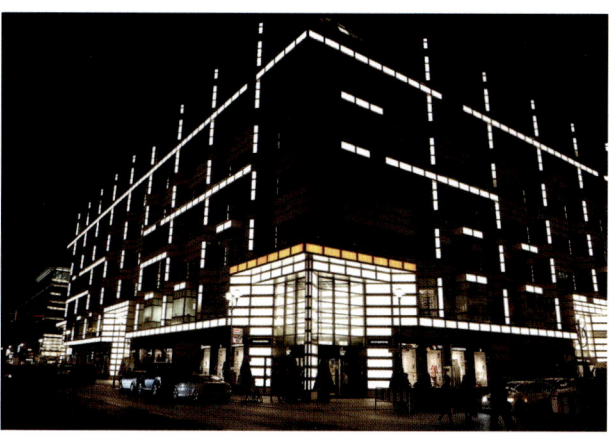

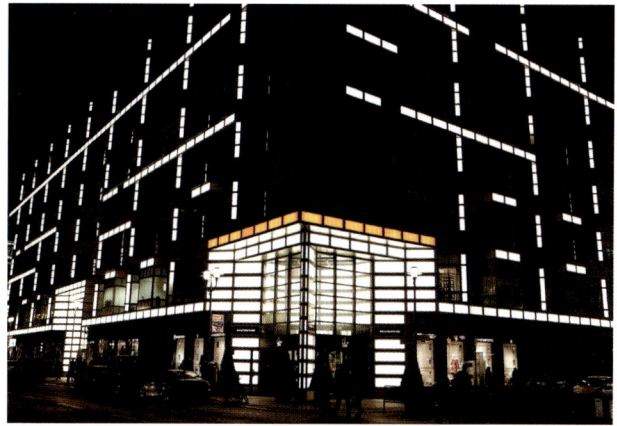

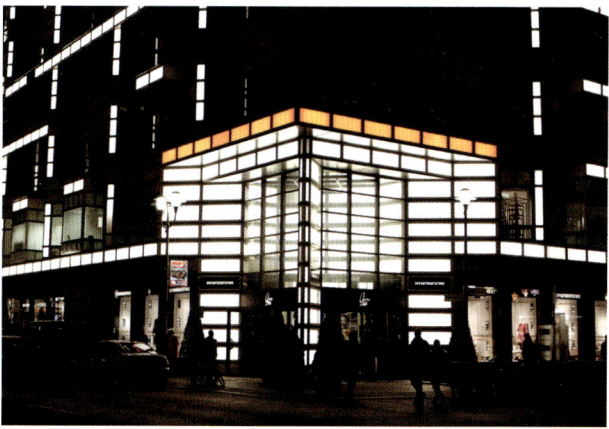

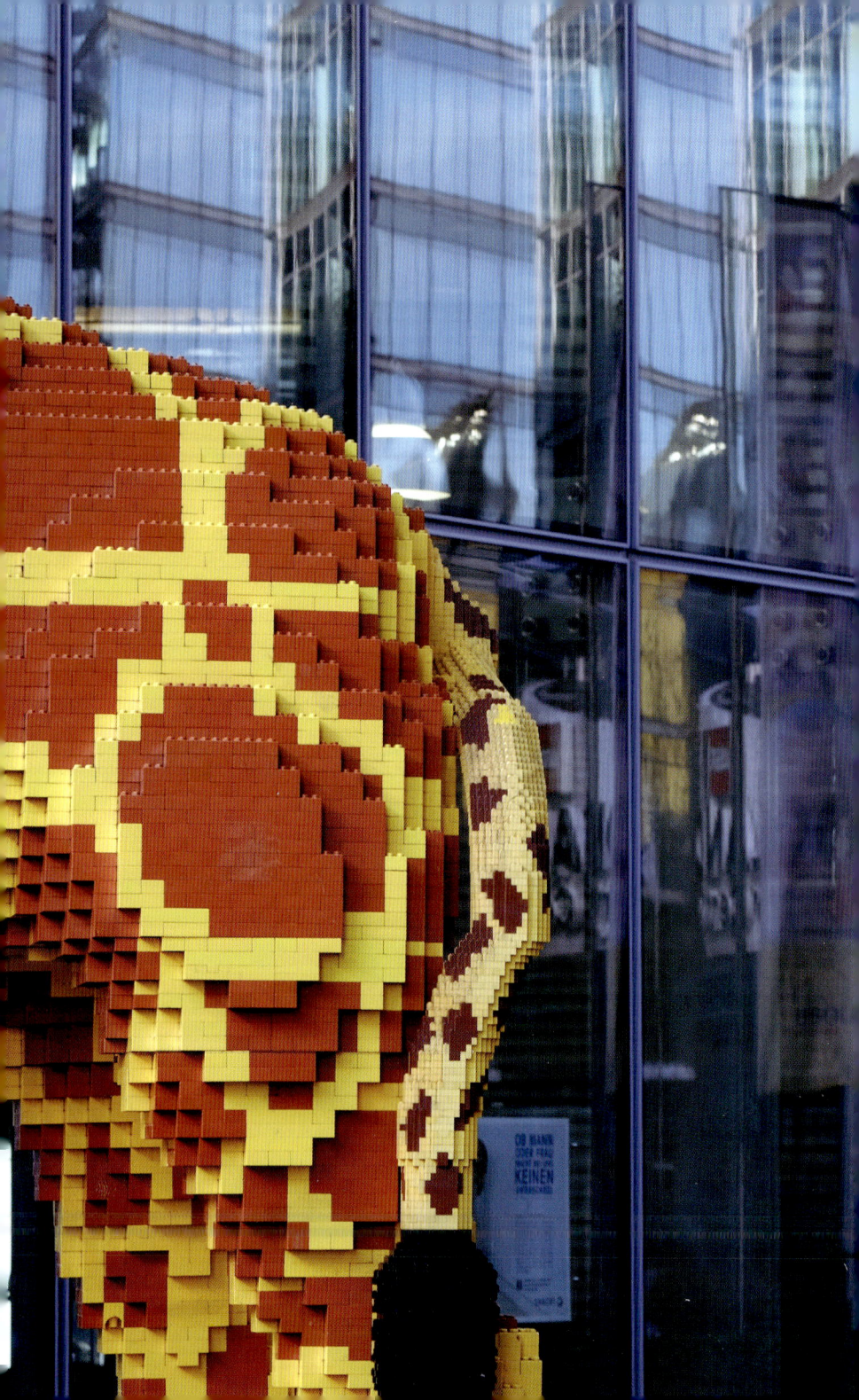

2.12 Shooting Video with the Fujifilm X100T

Professional filmmakers need the more robust optics of larger, more capable cameras, but no modern camera should be without the ability to quickly and easily shoot short videos.

X100T

The Movie Set-Up menu (Red 5.6) has settings for configuring the frame size and frame rate for your videos, as well as the light sensitivity and the microphone recording level.

The Fujifilm X100T shoots video in full HD (1080p) or HD at 60, 50, 30, 25, and 24 frames per second. Audio is recorded in stereo at 36 Mbps. You can also shoot while using the optical viewfinder.

You can adjust many parameters for shooting video, including the aperture, shutter speed, and ISO value. You can also choose a film simulation, which allows you to shoot video in black-and-white. You can use continuous focusing or manual focusing with focus peaking. The camera also features a 2.5mm stereo microphone jack and an HDMI port for hooking the camera up to an external monitor or television.

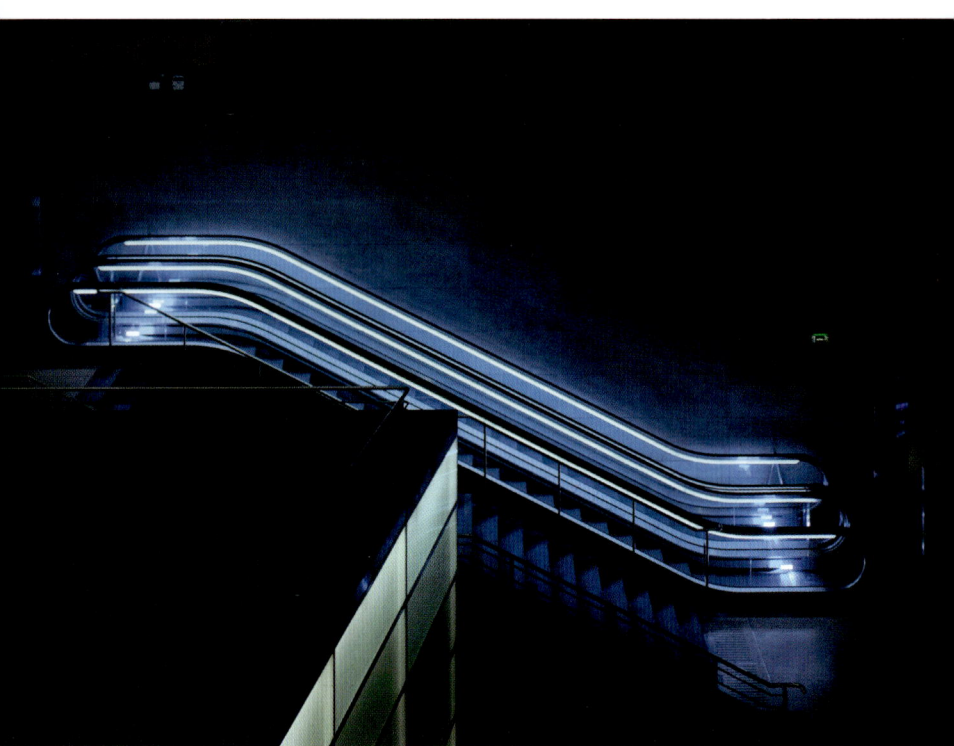

3 CREATIVE PHOTOGRAPHY WITH THE X100T AND X100S

I think the X100 series cameras are best suited for photographing people, events, landscapes, urban architecture, street life, and evening scenes. The characteristics of these cameras make them particularly suited for situations when it is undesirable to carry heavy equipment. Another reason the X100T has become my daily companion is that it fits in nearly any jacket pocket. In chapter 4, "Accessories," I'll talk more about portability and discuss what to include in the perfect gear bag.

In science, the simple act of taking a measurement may influence the results of an experiment. In photography, a similar phenomenon can happen when potential subjects realize you're pointing a camera in their direction—they either turn away or deliberately smile at the camera, and the photographic moment evaporates. Photographing models or people who gladly ham it up for the camera results in a different type of image. Capturing an authentic moment with genuine feeling and atmosphere requires subtle, inconspicuous, and quiet work. This is where the Fujifilm X100T and X100S shine. Because the cameras are small and inconspicuous, I can engage with subjects more thoroughly and often elicit a genuine questioning nod or a warm, friendly smile. The dialog is primarily between two people, and the camera becomes less of a threat. Because the operation of the camera is so intuitive and is reduced to the most essential functions, I can focus on when to release the shutter instead of battling with excessive technology. For all these reasons, the Fujifilm X100 series has earned a cultlike following among street photographers. My friend sums up the delightful process of working with this camera series: "The camera is effectively an extension of my right eye."

What follows are concrete examples that tease out the strengths of the Fujifilm X100T and X100S, along with explanations about how I approach specific shooting scenarios.

SCENARIO 1: STEALTH OPS (SILENT SHOOTING)

A client hired me to shoot a series of photos in a small Parisian theater and asked me to expressively document the actors, the ambience, and the play itself, as well as an outdoor portrait of the playwright. The theater was cramped and dark, and the first row of spectators was positioned near the stage. The lighting was minimal and primarily illuminated the stage actors. For my first attempt, I wanted to photograph during an actual performance of the play to avoid images that felt contrived. The shutter noise of my Fujifilm X-Pro1 would have been much too loud and distracting, but the nearly silent shutter of the X100S allowed me to photograph during the play without disturbing the spectators or the actors. The lighting conditions required that I shoot with ISO sensitivities between 5000 and 6400, so the camera's low-noise performance at higher ISO values and fast lens worked in my favor. To avoid motion blur while I shot the actors on stage, I set the shutter speed to 1/60 second and I left the aperture at f/2 or f/2.8 because of the dim light. I decided to underexpose my images by 1 to 1 2/3 stops so I could capture the atmosphere of the scene; the exposure compensation dial allowed me to change this setting while I kept the camera to my eye. Auto ISO ensured that my exposures were balanced and even.

NOTE

Working with a tripod would have been too distracting, so I chose a tool that I recommend in all my workshops: a string tripod. It is nothing more than a piece of common string or twine attached to a tripod plate at one end. I stand on the loose end of the string and steady the camera by pulling the string tight. The camera can still be moved laterally, but slight vertical shifts are mostly eliminated. If you don't need to adjust your camera vertically, this makeshift tool may be a better solution than a monopod.

I fixed the white balance and set the exposure meter to average with the goal of producing a balanced, color-neutral exposure.

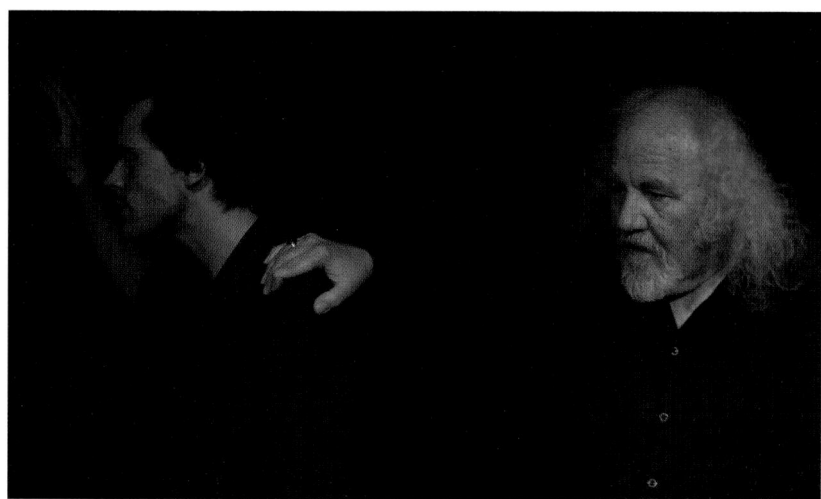

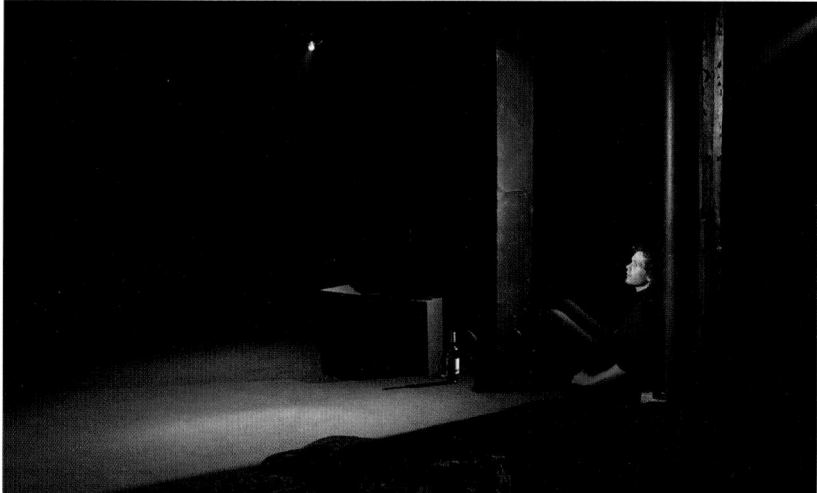

Figure 3.1: Scenes in a dimly lit theater

Focus method	AF-S, single frame, center AF field
Exposure	Manual, f/2–2.8, 1/60 second, ISO 4000–6400
White balance	Manual, fixed setting
Notes	Fujifilm X100S, stealth photography

Table 3.1: Exposure details for scenes in a dimly lit theater

SCENARIO 2: STREET PHOTOGRAPHY

Street photography involves capturing life on the street spontaneously and organically. The best street photographs are as authentic as possible and are void of artificial intervention or contrivance. If you fiddle with your camera too long, you'll miss the moment, especially when people are key elements of your composition. You need to react and focus quickly. I use a broad range of ISO values for this type of photography (e.g., ISO 200–1600 during the day and ISO 200–4000 at night), which allows me to handle a variety of lighting conditions. I also use a fairly fast shutter speed (e.g., 1/250 second) so I can freeze movement in my images even when I'm on the go. The key challenge is focusing. Depending on your speed or the speed of the subject, continuous autofocus (AF-C) with the Multi AF or Area mode is often a good choice. In AF-C mode, the camera constantly updates and refines the focus as long as the shutter button is pressed. The Multi AF mode, which is often called automatic tracking, will adjust the active AF field to follow the main subject as long as it retains enough contrast for the camera to detect it. These tools allow you to keep the image frame constant even while the subject changes position. Alternatively, you can use the Area AF mode to choose a specific AF field, establish focus on the main subject, then track the subject manually with the shutter button pressed halfway down. In both cases, the camera continuously updates the focus. With continuous shooting, or burst mode, you can capture either three or six frames per second (with the Low or High setting) while the focus keeps adjusting—a truly powerful feature. Make sure you have a fast memory card in your camera so the images can be saved quickly. I set up one of the seven shooting profiles on my camera for spontaneous street photography (Red 3.3).

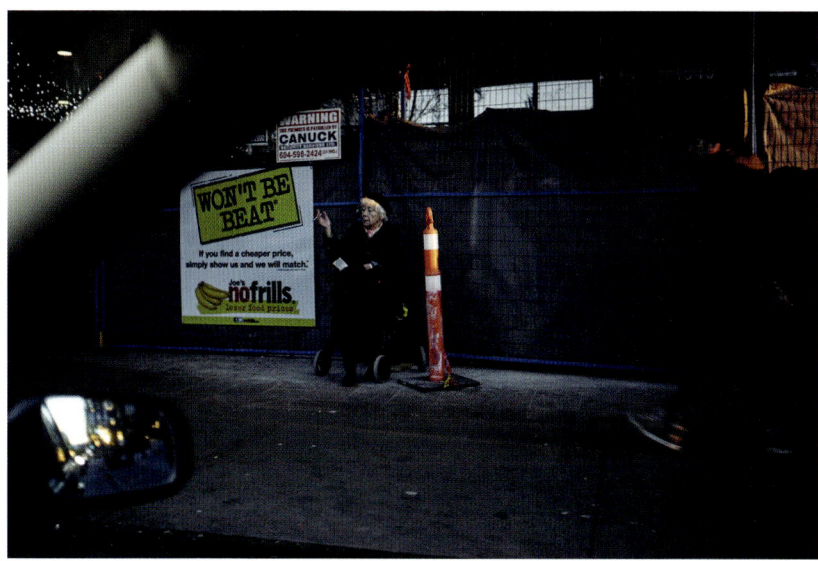

Figure 3.2: **A spontaneous street photography portrait.** © Kale Friesen

Focus method	AF-S, single frame, center AF field
Exposure	Manual, f/2, 1/55 second, ISO 400
White balance	Auto
Notes	Fujifilm X100T, camera handheld while driving

Table 3.2: **Exposure details for a spontaneous street photography portrait**

NOTE

Different places around the world have various laws and customs regarding photography of people in public places, such as on a regular city street. In Germany, for instance, a modification of a privacy law went into effect on January 27, 2015. Photographers may face criminal charges even for pressing the shutter button halfway in some circumstances. The relevant legislation was inconspicuously included in a law to prevent child pornography. The law makes it punishable to photograph "helpless people" in public. The ▶

rationale is that it will prevent violent perpetrators from photographing their victims with cell phones and publishing the images online. The law states that a prison sentence of up to two years or a fine will be imposed on anyone who captures, broadcasts, or transfers an image that depicts the helplessness of another person without authorization, thereby violating the privacy rights of the person depicted. If you encounter a homeless person sitting in front of a bank who is being ignored by people on the street as they rush past, you may have found a compelling image, but think twice about taking the shot. If you can prove that the photo is a part of a photo essay or project, or if you have a press pass, certain exceptions can be granted. Always use common sense when you weigh the pros and cons of shooting in these types of circumstances.

SCENARIO 3: CITYSCAPES

During a stopover in Paris, the Montmartre Cemetery presented countless photographic opportunities, all of which were easily within the technical capabilities of the Fujifilm X100T. The large cemetery is latticed with narrow paths and alleys. I wanted to spontaneously react to scenes as I saw them, so I didn't bother with my tripod. The overcast sky after a rain and the bright building facades in the background made a perfect optical counterweight to the dark and expressive tombs on either side of the cobblestones. I used the optical viewfinder to get the exact exposure I wanted; it's the ideal window for directly assessing your shooting environment. To prevent the highlights from clipping while I retained a good level of detail in the shadows, I slightly boosted the contrast range to DR 200%. The cobblestone path in the foreground that runs from the left of the frame toward the horizon was key to my composition, so I used my 28mm wide-angle conversion lens. Focus peaking made it easy to establish my desired depth of field because its colorful highlights identified the areas of the scene that were in focus. In addition to precisely choosing a focal plane, the ability to examine the depth of field in a scene is one of the main advantages of using manual focus.

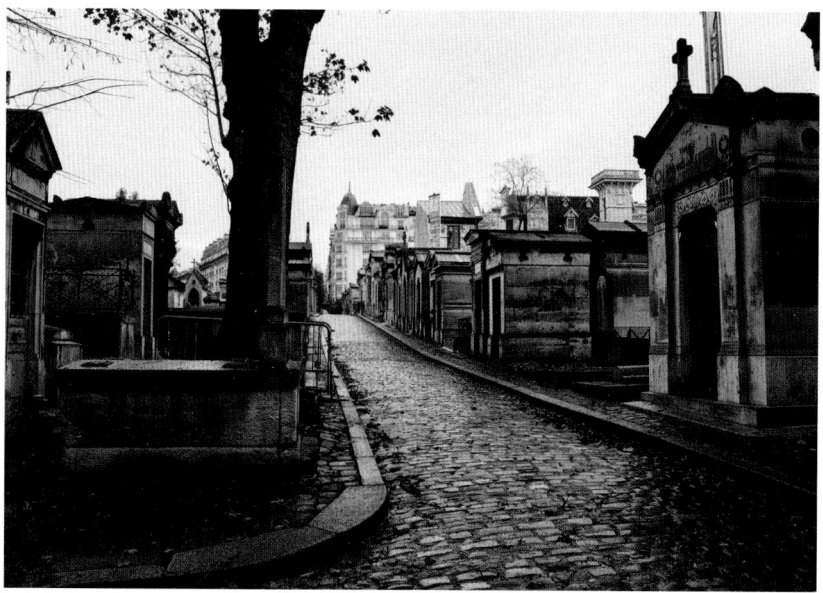

Figure 3.3: **Montmartre Cemetery, Paris**

Focus method	M, focus peaking, single frame
Exposure	Manual, f/8, 1/80 second, ISO 400
White balance	Auto
Contrast range	DR=200%
Film simulation	Monochrome with red filter
Notes	Fujifilm X100T, 28mm conversion lens

Table 3.3: **Exposure details for Montmartre Cemetery, Paris**

SCENARIO 4: SPONTANEOUS PORTRAIT

This picture was taken during a workshop. The idea for the portrait, which was taken on an escalator, was sparked by the way the neon lights along the handrail illuminated the woman's face. Thanks to a high ISO value and the wide aperture, a fast shutter speed of 1/250 second was possible, which froze all motion in the scene. Pictures like this rely mostly on the natural appearance of the subject—the position of her head and her natural smile. In situations like these, the intuitive operation of the Fujifilm X100 series cameras is a true advantage.

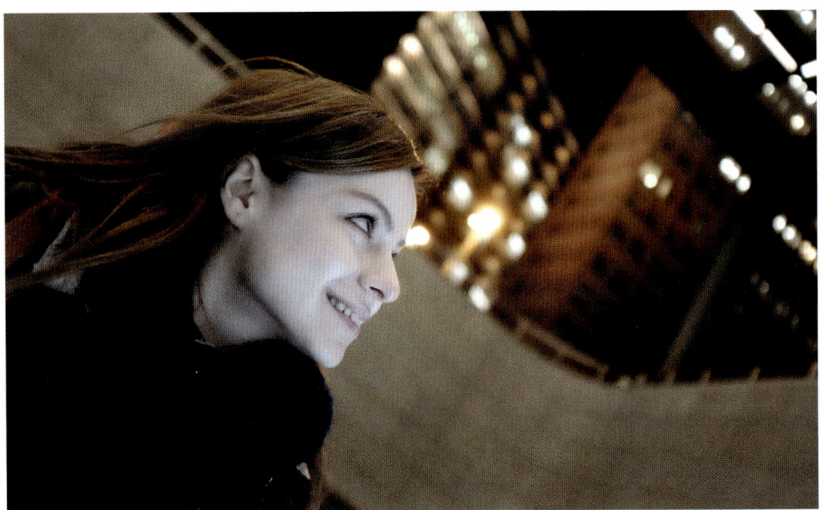

Figue 3.4: A portrait on location

Focus method	AF-S, single frame
Exposure	Manual, f/2, 1/250 second, ISO 6400 (Auto)
White balance	Auto
Contrast range	DR=200%
Film simulation	Classic Chrome
Notes	Fujifilm X100T

Table 3.4: Exposure details for shooting a portrait on location

It was quick and easy to set up the camera for this shot. In a single motion, I opened the aperture and set the shutter speed as I brought the camera to my eye and instantly composed the frame. The whole process took less than a second, thanks in part to having basic settings already programmed, including Auto ISO with a range of 200 to 6400, a minimum shutter speed of 1/60 second, autofocus enabled, and my desired film simulation. When you're prepared for a critical moment, you will have a greater opportunity to get the shot you want.

SCENARIO 5: SEARCHING FOR A LOCATION

The search for an ideal photo shoot location is a key part of a photographer's prep work. This is especially true in the fashion industry, where clients put lots of emphasis on the overall effect of an image. A stylish model is not enough. This picture was taken while the photographer, Kale Friesen, was taking test pictures in an industrial area of Vancouver, Canada. The monochromatic feel is the result of an overcast sky, the gray tones in the model's clothes, and the color of the wall behind him. The color saturation and white balance were adjusted during RAW conversion using Capture One Pro 8. The preset film simulations don't always match the client's or the photographer's vision, which is why having a RAW file as a starting point is so powerful for letting your creativity run wild.

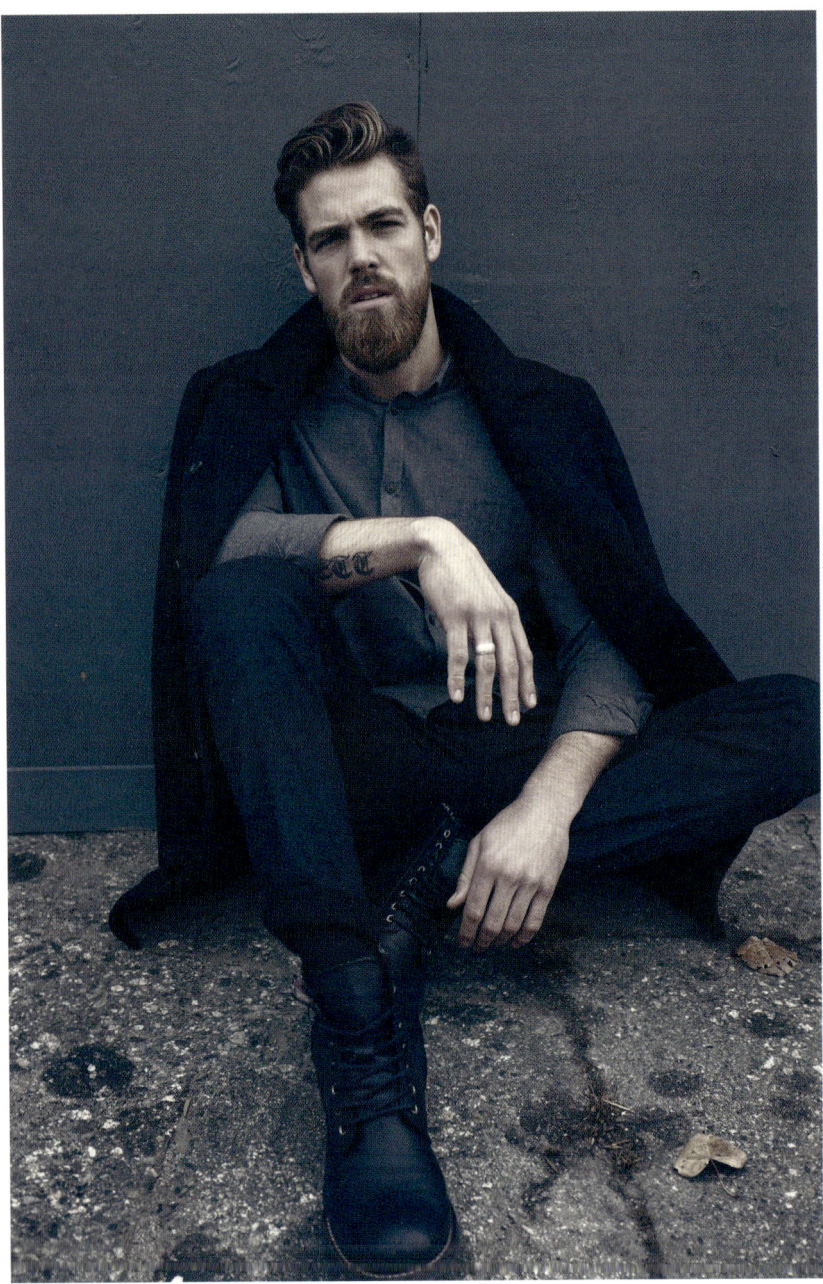

Figure 3.5: **Street portrait.** © Kale Friesen

Focus method	AF-S, single frame
Exposure	Manual, f/2, 1/1300 second, ISO 400
White balance	Manual
Notes	Fujifilm X100T, RAW conversion with Capture One Pro 8

Table 3.5: **Exposure details for street portrait**

SCENARIO 6: PARIS STREETS

The capital city of France is unquestionably a dream location for street photographers. Elliott Erwitt, an advertising and documentary photographer born in Paris, said: "For me, photography is the art of observation. It's about discovering something interesting in a conventional location." Being encumbered by a heavy equipment bag and a weighty camera hinders your ability to stay alert for the right moment. For me, the main thrill is scanning my environment—either through the viewfinder or simply with my eyes—as I search for subjects. Often, when I photograph in these situations, I set up my camera before I head out, then I wait until the end of the day or when I'm back at my hotel to view my work. Constantly looking at your camera monitor will prevent you from spotting fleeting moments. Set the ISO to Auto (e.g., ISO 200–3200) and the minimum shutter speed to 1/125 second to ensure that your images will be properly exposed.

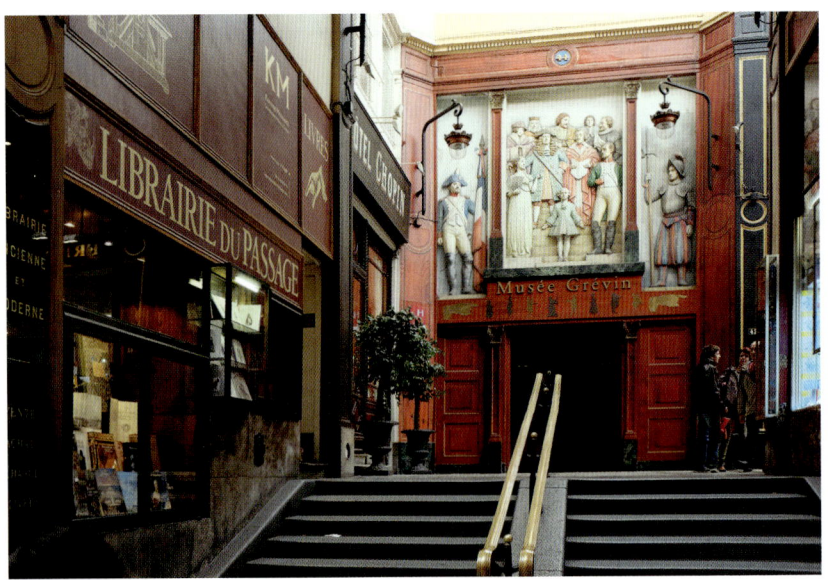

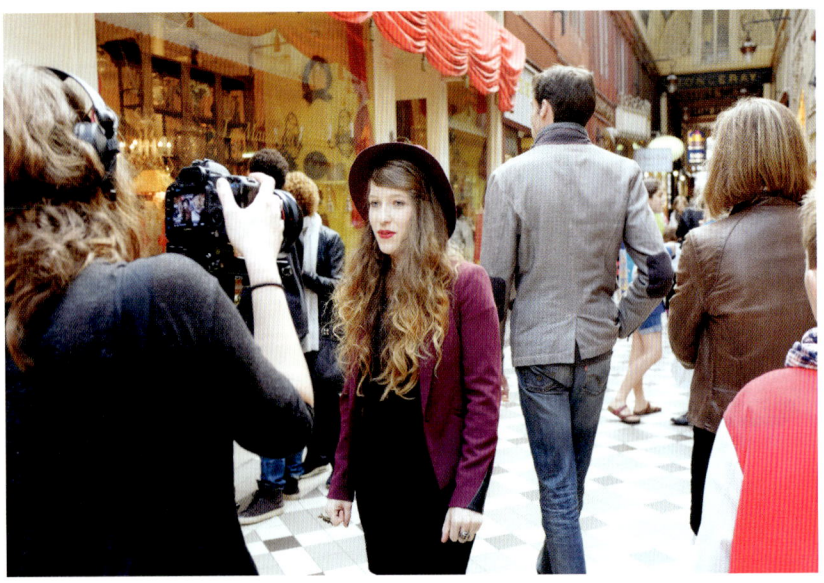

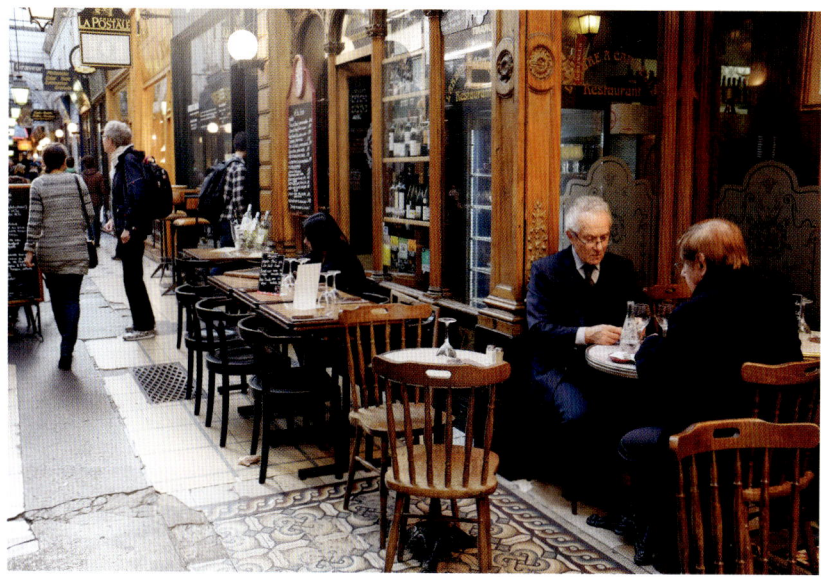

Figure 3.6: **Street life in Paris**

Focus method	AF-S, single frame
Exposure	Manual, f/4, 1/125 second, ISO 1600–2000 (Auto)
White balance	Manual
Film simulation	Provia
Notes	Fujifilm X100S, Auto ISO

Table 3.6: **Exposure details for street life in Paris**

Some photographs turn out best when they're shot blind, which is how I shot the picture of the café. Instead of looking through the viewfinder, I held the camera at stomach level and pointed it in the right direction. In less than a second I had captured the image I wanted as I passed by. To protect my camera from danger amid the masses and to keep it securely on my body, I use a hand strap that will prevent it from slipping from my hands. It also thwarts pickpockets.

SCENARIO 7: CYBORG GIRL STUDIO PORTRAIT

People often ask me if the small Fujifilm cameras can be used in a studio with an artificial lighting system. The answer, not surprisingly, is a definite yes. As in so many other situations, the Fujifilm X100 series cameras excel in part because of their modest appearance. Studio photo shoots are full of equipment—tripods, lights, accessories galore—and extra personnel, including assistants, make-up artists, and others. Amid the chaos, the person being photographed tends to get tense. One of the photographer's most important jobs is to put the subject at ease and create a laid-back atmosphere that is conducive to relaxed poses. Using a small camera is helpful because it facilitates more eye contact between the photographer and the subject. To produce a detail-rich image with a perfectly lit backdrop, I planned in advance to shoot this portrait in black-and-white with manually defined settings for the aperture, shutter speed, and ISO. The lighting setup consisted of two lights: one main light with a small softbox (16 x 24 inches) pointed at the model, and one light fitted with a snoot to direct light at the subject's arm. A quick series of test shots helped me decide how to regulate the flash power settings. I used a tripod with an Arca-Swiss ball head mount. The Fujifilm MHG-X100 handgrip has tripod threads, so an additional tripod plate is not necessary.

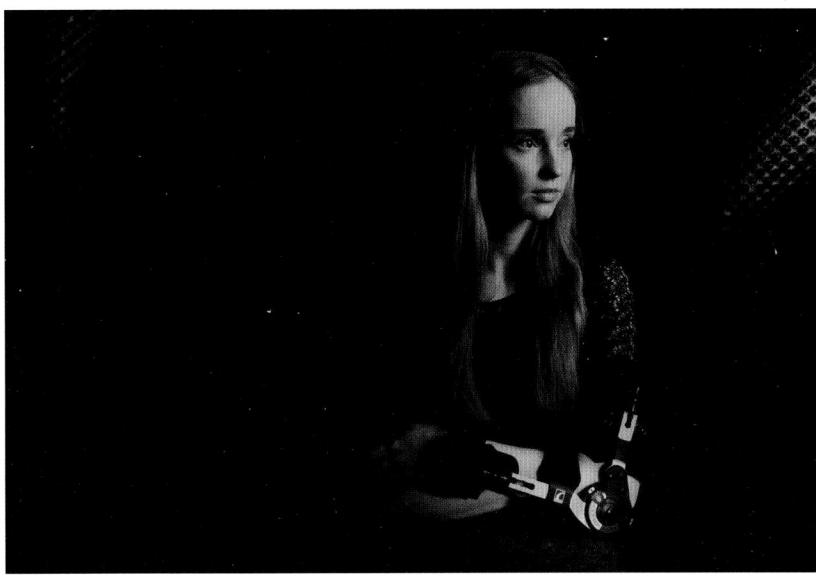

Figure 3.7: **Studio portrait**

Focus method	Manual, single frame
Exposure	Manual, f/2.8, 1/80 second, ISO 1250
White balance	Manual
Film simulation	Monochrome with red filter, shadows and highlights +2
Notes	Fujifilm X100T, studio flash units

Table 3.7: **Exposure details for studio portrait**

Because the physical dimensions of the Fujifilm X100 series cameras are so small, you can carry out experiments that you otherwise wouldn't be able to do, such as placing the camera in a rounded glass bowl. The photograph in figure 3.8 was created with this approach. The camera and the bowl were moved until the desired effect was achieved.

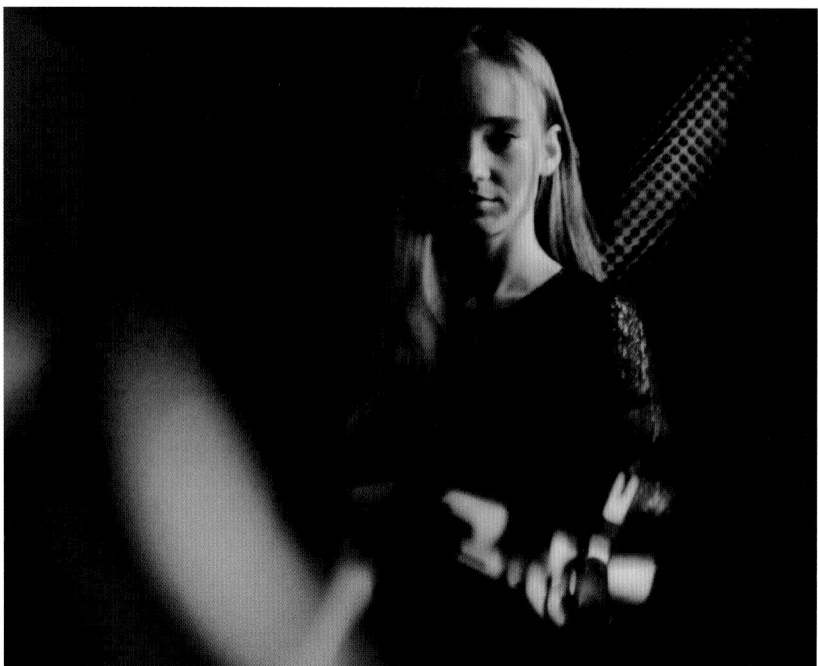

Figure 3.8: Creative photography using diverse props, such as a glass bowl

Unmounted lenses, eyeglasses, magnifying glasses, and so forth lend themselves to experiments like this. You can find them for little to no money in secondhand stores and at flea markets.

SCENARIO 8: ARCHITECTURAL PHOTOGRAPHY

Meticulously composing an image to bring out the best in your subject can be very satisfying, and the Fujifilm X100T has a big, bright viewfinder that makes it all the more enjoyable. Even though architectural photographers place a premium on framing images with certain proportions, such as the golden ratio (in which a distance is divided into two unequal parts, and the smaller part relates to the larger part at the same ratio as the larger part relates to the full distance), sometimes a clean geometric division of the image area and its key elements produces a satisfying and solid composition.

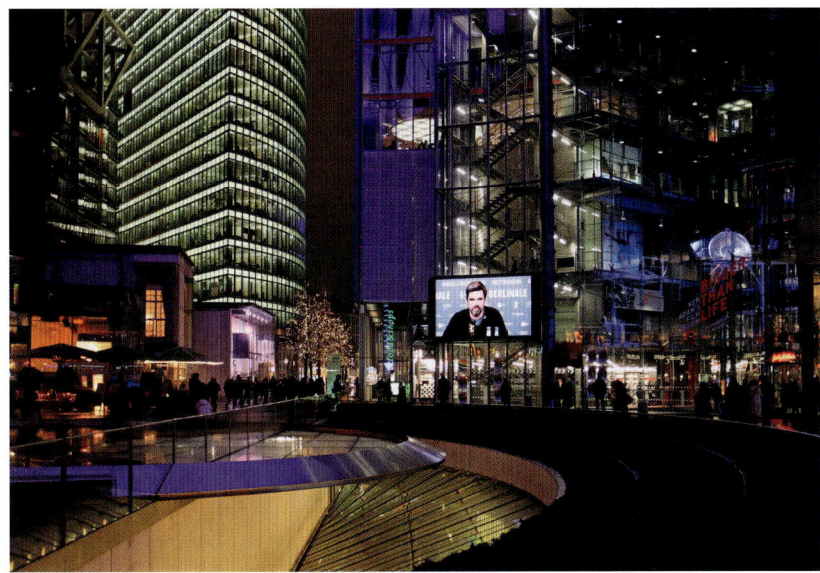

Figure 3.9: **Urban architecture, Sony Center, Berlin**

Focus method	Manual, single frame
Exposure	Manual, f/2, 1/20 second, ISO 640
White balance	Auto
Film simulation	Provia
Notes	Fujifilm X100T

Table 3.8: **Exposure details for urban architecture, Sony Center, Berlin**

The image in figure 3.9 was taken with the X100T's 23mm (35mm equivalent) focal length lens. Even with a wide-angle lens it is nearly impossible to capture the entire structure of the distinctive dome, let alone the other buildings that make up the complex. When you look at the scene without a camera, you have to turn your head from one side to the other, so framing the image for a photograph is a real challenge. The task here was to find a partial view of the scene that conveys a sense of the whole, which is why the wide-angle conversion lens was not used. In the following paragraph I discuss the composition of the image with the help of green guiding lines and other marks in red and yellow. The image is divided vertically into thirds and horizontally into fourths, with an additional optical center axis.

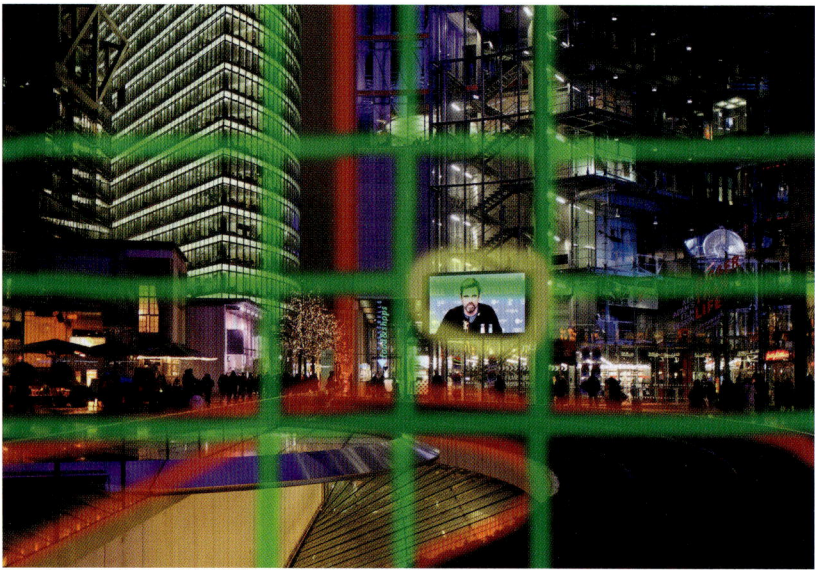

Figure 3.10: Image analysis, Sony Center, Berlin

The green lines produce four small squares in the center of the image. In the lower-left quadrant, all the key lines of the image converge (marked in red). This point of convergence, in combination with the giant video screen in the lower-right square, form the center of the photograph. The curved lines in the lower portion of the image (marked in red) exit the image area at the intersections of the dividing lines. The brighter and darker quadrants are diagonally opposite from each other. Finding the perfect vantage point was relatively easy using the Framing Guideline for the viewfinder (Blue 2.3.10). There are several framing grids available: Grid 9, Grid 24, and HD Framing. Grid 9 follows the rule of thirds and superimposes a nine-box grid over the image area; Grid 24 superimposes a symmetrical 6 x 4 grid; and HD Framing provides guidelines for composing an image in HD format.

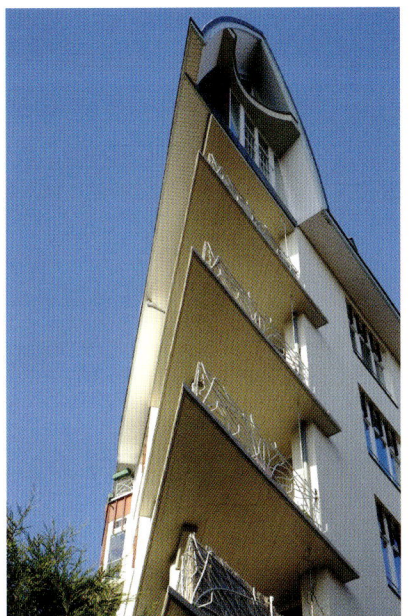 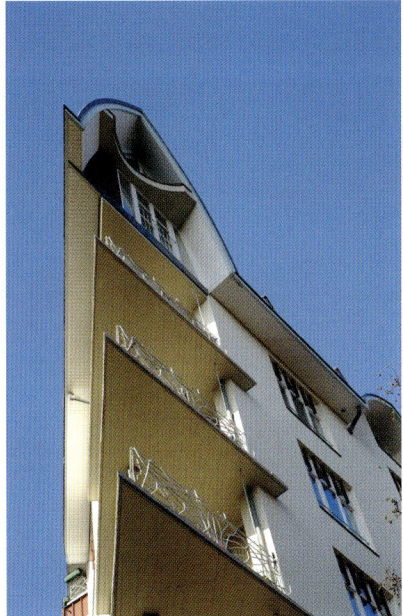

Figure 3.11: **Positioning the camera to avoid converging vertical lines**

Deliberately tilting the camera is one way to avoid converging vertical lines. You can use the vertical lines in a framing grid to tilt the camera and align vertical lines in the scene. This approach helps make architectural images feel more relaxed, but it is a stopgap measure, not a definitive solution.

Before I conclude this section on creative photography, I want to mention a special technique that addresses the desire for even higher image resolution. If Fujifilm were to release a new camera with upwards of 60 megapixels, it would be a dream come true for landscape and architectural photographers. But what if you already own a camera with that capability? The goal here is "super-resolution," and the process starts with using your camera's burst mode and shooting 10 to 20 images of the same subject while handholding the camera so that each image is slightly different due to subtle shifts in camera position. A tiny detail in the scene would be captured by neighboring pixels from frame to frame. In contrast to a single exposure, which requires the interpolation of red, green, and blue pixels to reproduce the actual color, you now have multiple exposures with pixels that recorded the identical detail in red, green, and blue.

After you shoot the pictures, follow this process: Stack the 20 images in Photoshop, then magnify the image by 200% (Resample Method: Nearest Neighbor). Automatically align the images, then set the opacity for the images from bottom to top at the following levels, with the fade blending mode set to Normal:

100%, 50%, 33%, 25%, 20%, 17%, 14%, 12%, 11%, 10%, 9%, 8%, 8%, 7%, 7%, 6%, 6%, 6%, 5%, 5%.

The next step is to sharpen the image with the following settings: Filter > Smart Sharpen, Amount = 300%, Radius = 2 pixels, Reduce Noise = 0%. The final step is to reduce everything to one layer and save it in your desired file format.

Be aware that this process takes a lot of computer processing power, and it can take up to an hour even with a fast computer. It's not practical to use this process for moving subjects because it's impossible to overlay multiple images without ghosting or artifacts. You'll find a much more exhaustive description of the process, including several examples, on Ian Norman's website (see the Photon Collective link in chapter 5).

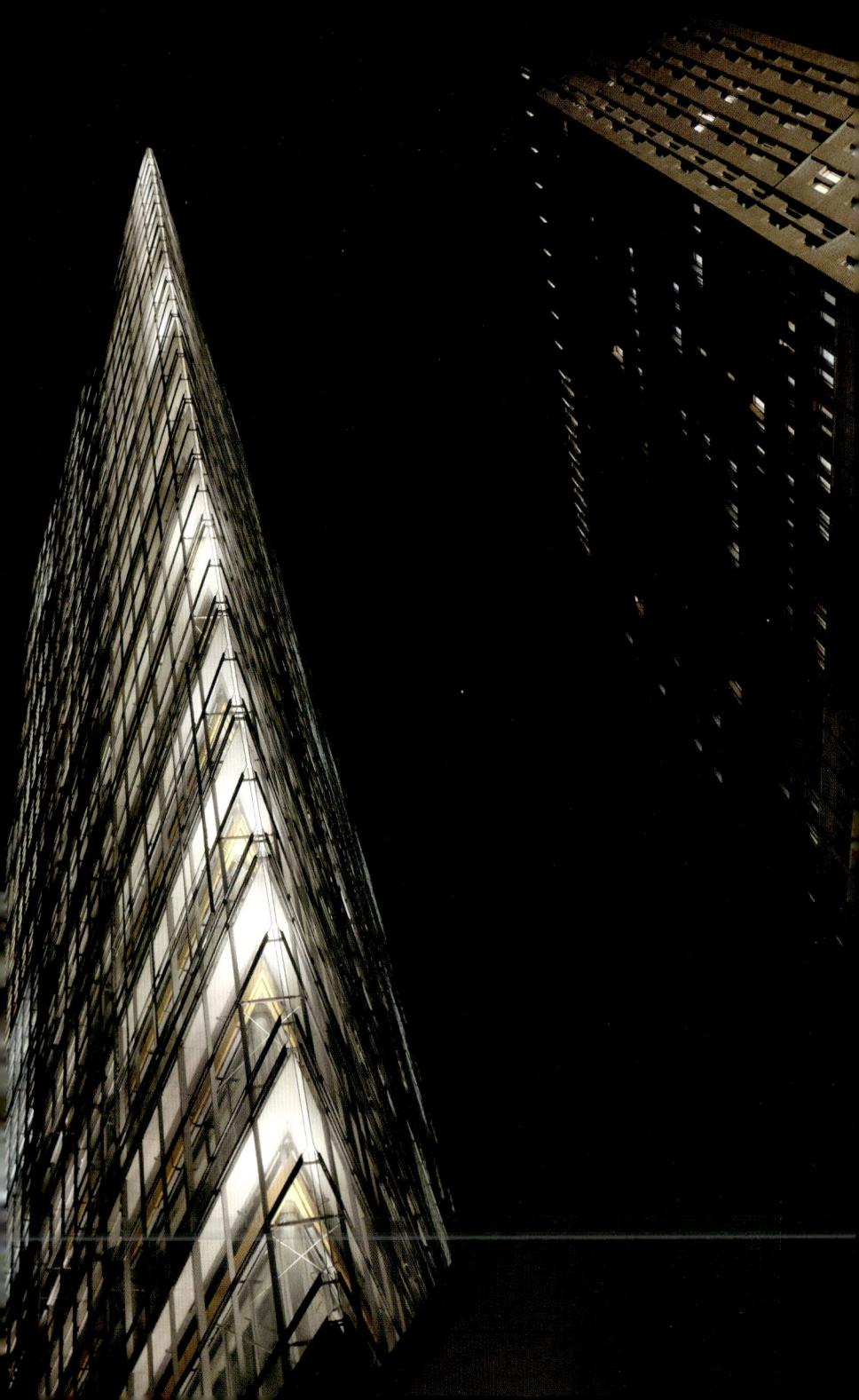

3.1 Which Camera Model Is Right for Me?

Much like giving advice about what kind of car to buy, it's hard to say which camera model is right for you. It just depends. The good news, however, is that regardless of whether you buy the X100T or X100S, you'll have a great camera. Both cameras have the same lens, the same X-Trans sensor and image processor, and produce the same high-quality pictures. And that means you can't argue the pros and cons of each model for the most important consideration: making great images. The cameras are also nearly identical in dimension, weight, and handling. As is always the case, though, better is the enemy of good.

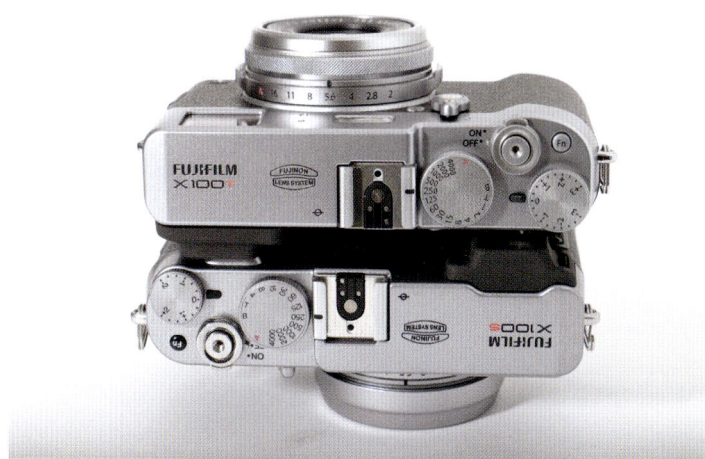

Figure 3.12: The Fujifilm X100S and X100T

In addition to the publicized improvements and developments of the X100T—including the electronic rangefinder and the electronic shutter with speeds up to

1/32,000 second—the arrangement and functionality of the buttons and dials were also updated, and the Q menu is more customizable.

You operate the buttons and dials mostly with your left and right thumbs. In my opinion, the new arrangement of the control keys on the X100T and the decision to replace what was a somewhat fiddly dial with four selector keys significantly improves the operation of the X100T.

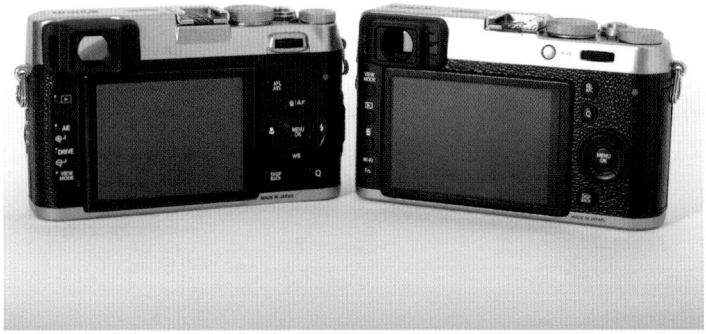

Figure 3.13: Comparison of the controls on the X100S (left) and the X100T (right)

On the X100T, a full dial has replaced the push-pull toggle switch, and the Drive button has been moved to the left of the command dial. The Q button that launches the Q menu is now logically positioned directly below the AEL/AFL button, which is in the same location along with the Display/Back button. The left side of the back is noticeably sleeker, with the following buttons arranged from top to bottom: View Mode to cycle through options for the viewfinder, LCD monitor, and eye sensor; the Playback button; the Delete button; and the Wi-Fi button. When the camera is in shooting mode, the bottom two buttons are programmable. In total, the X100T has seven programmable function buttons (the X100S has one programmable function key next to the shutter button on top of the camera). This wealth of function buttons, combined with the fully programmable Q menu, makes customization a key emphasis of the X100T. I would like to see a firmware update that allows photographers to save all settings on an SD card so they can transfer them from one camera to another. Users could even create a database for different shooting circumstances.

The differences between the Fujifilm X100T and X100S are probably not large enough to warrant upgrading from one to the other, but if you're new to these delightful cameras, it makes sense to start with the most recent version. Anyone who is familiar with Fujifilm and the frequency of their firmware updates knows that older models are never forgotten. In most cases, you need only to have a bit of patience to work with the new Classic Chrome film simulation on the X100S. But if patience isn't your thing, try the following tip:

X100S

If you have the Fujifilm X100S, you can edit the EXIF data for your images (essentially altering the metadata to match the X100T) to unlock the Classic Chrome simulation in a RAW converter.

4 ACCESSORIES

Accessories often make life easier and can turn your camera into an even more user-friendly tool. Because Fujifilm cameras are so popular, there is no shortage of gadgets on the market. I'll discuss a few of them here, focusing on products I've tested myself.

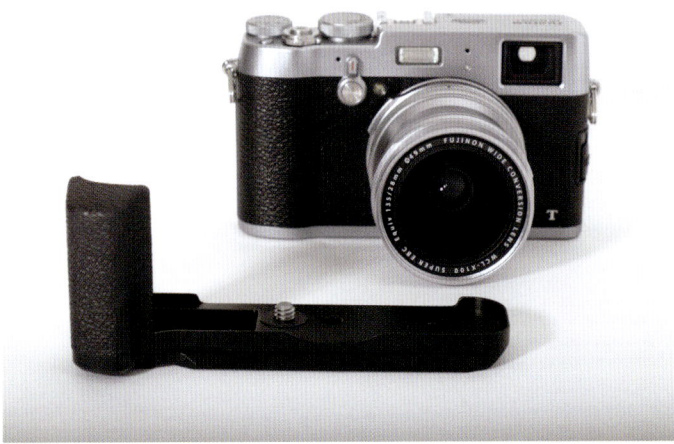

Figure 4.1: Fujifilm handgrip MHG-X100

Taking pictures is more enjoyable when you have a firm grip on your camera and can operate the controls smoothly, which is why I always use a handgrip when I shoot with the Fujifilm X-Series cameras. The Fujifilm MHG-X100 works perfectly. It is compatible with Arca-Swiss tripod heads without an adapter plate; the clamping mechanism of the tripod head engages directly with the grip attachment.

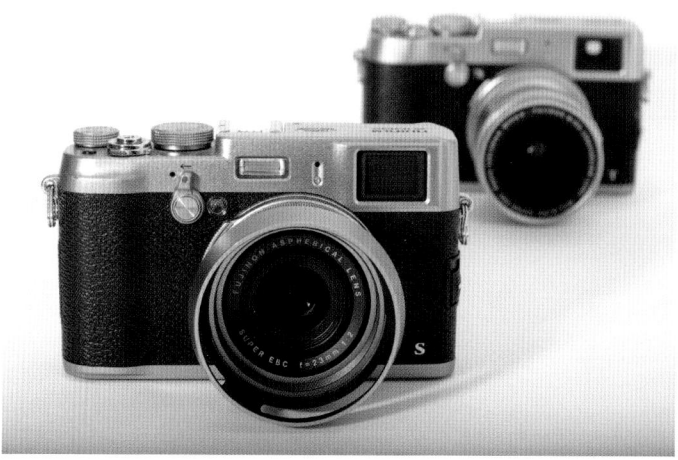

Figure 4.2: Lens hood for the X100 series

The Fujifilm LH-X100 lens hood is compatible with all three of the X100 series cameras. In addition to its primary function of preventing incident light from entering the lens and producing unwanted flare and reflections in your image, it also protects the lens.

I can't tell you how many times I've watched the following scenario play out in camera stores: A customer has just picked out a high-quality camera and lens, and before the salesperson can lead him or her to the checkout counter, the customer is already talking about needing protective filters. I don't think additional glass surfaces can improve image quality. High-end filters are optically superior, of course, but you should use filters only when they serve a specific purpose for your photography, such as with polarizers and ND filters. However, you can use any filter that has a 49mm diameter with the X100 series cameras. The Seven5 system from Lee Filters is an elegant solution for your filter needs (see chapter 5, "Links"). The system has three parts: the adapter ring that screws onto the lens, the filter holder that attaches to

the adapter, and the filter that slides into the holder. You
can fit up to three filters in the holder at once.

The selection for camera straps is seemingly endless.
I tend to avoid straps that have bold, conspicuous lettering
on them and opt for understated straps that attract less at-
tention. For years I've been a big fan of the camera straps
and clips from Peak Design (see chapter 5, "Links"). The
company's products are made from high-quality materials;
they are developed by photographers, for photographers;
and they are highly customizable, thanks to an ingenious
clasp system.

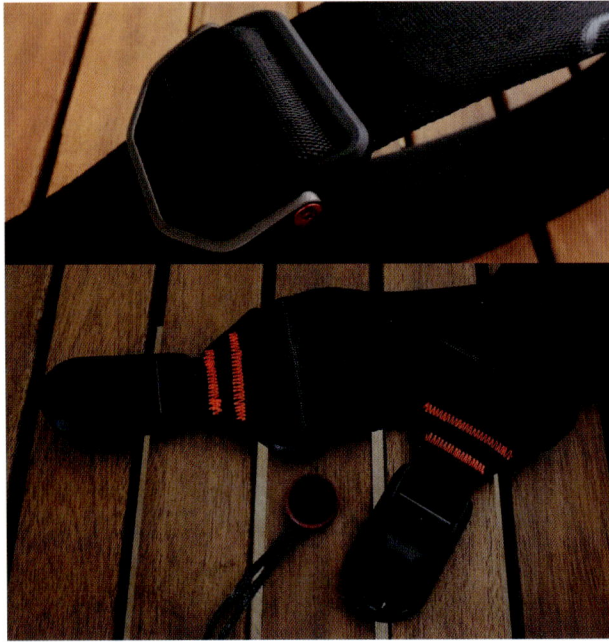

Figure 4.3: Peak
Design camera
strap

It seems that a perfect gear bag is always a work in
progress, partially because your collection of equipment changes over time. Furthermore, your equipment
needs vary for each photographic excursion. You can find

countless bags, backpacks, and combinations thereof in all imaginable shapes, sizes, and price ranges. At one point, my collection had become quite impressive, but I never seemed to find the perfect fit. Eventually I discovered that I could convert one of my general purpose bags into a customized photo bag by using a camera case insert. It offers the best of both worlds—totally inconspicuous from the outside, and perfectly designed for my photographic needs on the inside. It is also a relatively affordable solution—most camera case inserts cost between $15 and $30, including the one I chose from ONA (see chapter 5, "Links"). As for the main bag to use with an insert, it's likely you already have something that will work.

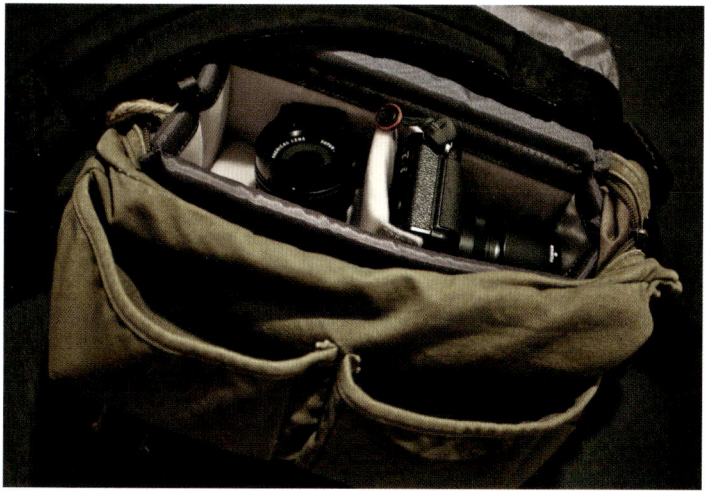

Figure 4.4: A camera bag insert from ONA that works with any general purpose bag

Photographers who travel have special packing requirements. I put my Fujifilm X100T, both conversion lenses (28mm and 50mm), the Lee filter system, and three fully charged batteries in my travel pack. If you use

Apple products, you likely have a power plug adapter that fits into the original Fujifilm battery charger, which is a more compact option than packing the cumbersome power cord. To take care of data safety and backup, I pack several smaller SD cards (e.g. 8 GB cards) and an external hard drive, ideally with an SD card reader. Including a laptop has obvious advantages, including being able to view, edit, and send images while on location, but it also makes your gear heavier and bulkier.

Other small but useful objects you might want to pack include a microfiber cloth, a small bellows, and a pack of silica gel to safeguard your equipment against moisture if you're headed to a humid climate. Include a stash of business cards, because meeting new people is part of travel and travel photography. You might consider packing a mobile printer, such as the Fujifilm Instax SHARE SP-1, so you can give a print to the people you photograph. It weighs about 9 ounces, measures roughly 4 x 5 x 1.5 inches, and operates on a battery. Creating a print and giving it to your subject is a lovely gesture of thanks that can bring real joy. In some cases you may be giving a person the first photo of him- or herself that was ever taken.

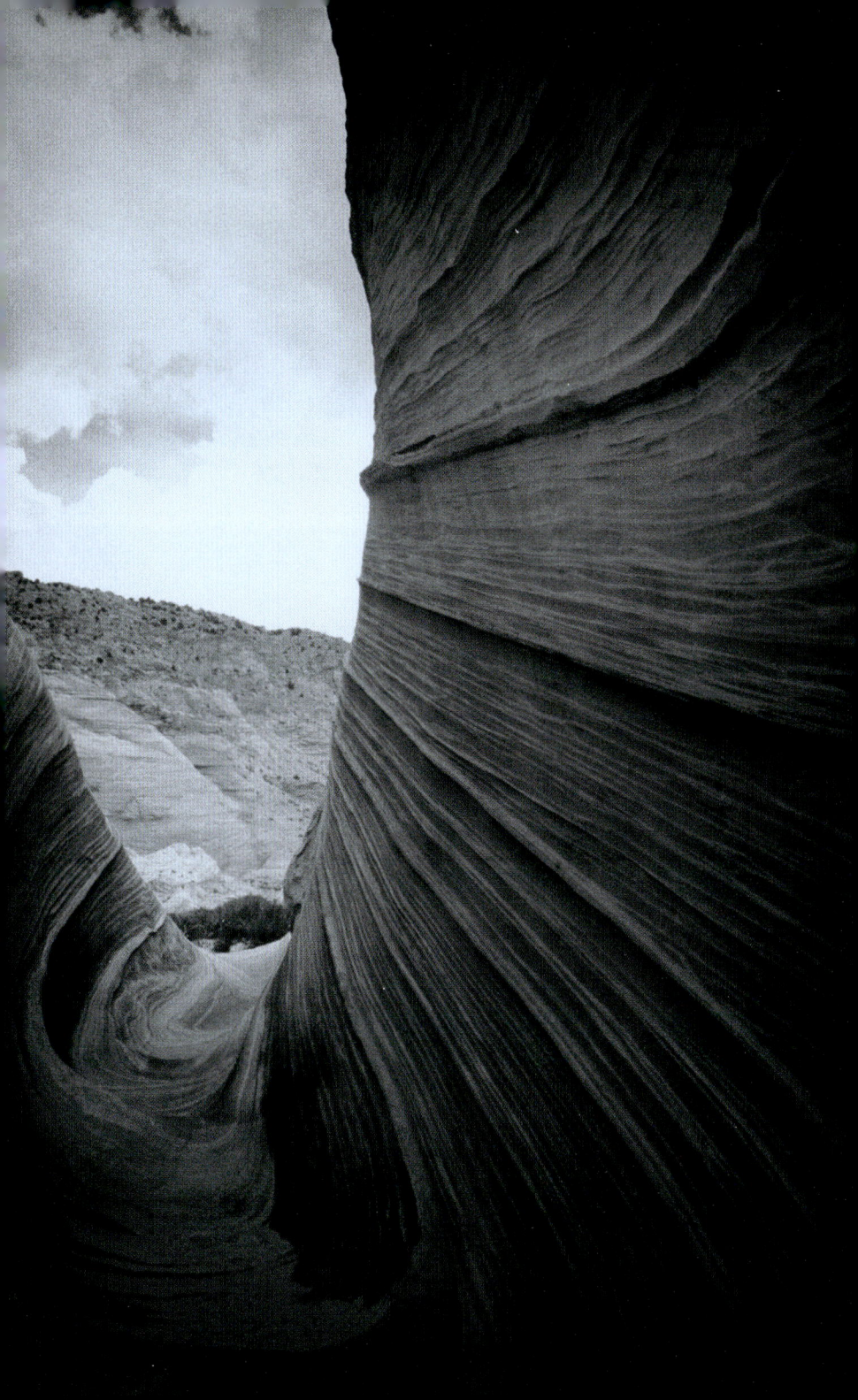

5 LINKS

Capture One Pro (RAW conversion software)
🌐 www.captureone.com

Fauland Photography School
🌐 school.fauland-photography.com

Fuji Rumors
🌐 www.fujirumors.com

Fujifilm firmware updates
🌐 www.fujifilm.com/support/digital_cameras/software

Fujifilm Instax SHARE SP-1 printer
🌐 www.fujifilm.com/products/instant_photo/printers/
instax_share_sp_1

Fujifilm USA
🌐 www.fujifilmusa.com

Fujifilm X100S instruction manual
🌐 www.fujifilm.com/support/digital_cameras/manuals/pdf/
index/x/fujifilm_x100s_manual_en.pdf

Fujifilm X100T instruction manual
🌐 fujifilm-dsc.com/en/manual/x100t/index.html

Lee Filters
🌐 www.leefilters.com

ONA (camera bag inserts)
🌐 www.onabags.com

Peak Design (camera straps)

🌐 peakdesign.com

Photo Ninja (RAW conversion software)

🌐 www.picturecode.com/download.php

**The Photon Collective: Super-Resolution Tutorial
by Ian Norman**

🌐 photoncollective.com/enhance-practical-superresolution-
in-adobe-photoshop

Silkypix (RAW conversion software)

🌐 www.silkypix.us

6 FINAL THOUGHTS

The modern era of digital photography is fast paced. Information that is current at this writing may be outdated by the time you read this book. To provide the latest news and tips, I set up a website that I continually update. If you're curious about the absolute latest developments for the Fujifilm X100 series cameras, please visit:

🌐 x100.fauland-photography.com

I use my Fujifilm X100 series camera nearly every day, and occasionally I post tips and tricks that you may find interesting and useful. Comments, questions, and suggestions are always welcome, and I'll do my best to answer any questions you have.

In a recent interview, I was asked what is so special to me about these Fujifilm cameras. Here is my response:

Over the years, I've used many different cameras and systems, and some have impressed me more than others. Aside from developing exciting new technology, such as the X-Trans sensor and a superb lens, Fujifilm has succeeded in building a camera with a soul that makes taking pictures a special experience. The last time I felt this way about a camera was when I shot with a Leica IIIf that my grandfather gave me. Any time it's possible to establish a connection with an object or a thing, your attitude about it changes, and this emotional element of taking pictures can alter the way you work. In other words, you're not going to end up with a better picture because you're shooting with a camera that squeezed an extra megapixel onto the sensor, but if you have a different feeling while you're shooting, you'll view your subjects differently. And if you're lucky, differently *will also mean* better. *I experience a significantly greater number of these moments when I shoot now.*

I wish you all the best with your Fujifilm X100—
whether it's the T or the S model—and may your light
always be good.

I'd like to thank Kale Friesen for allowing me to use two
of his images (figures 3.2 and 3.5). Thank you also to
Martin Vieten (figure 2.10).

INDEX

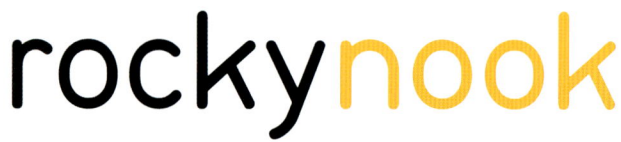
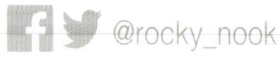